100 MOST DANGEROUS THINGS ON THE PLANET

Conceived, edited, and designed by Marshall Editions
The Old Brewery
6 Blundell Street
London N7 9BH

ISBN-13: 978-0-545-06927-4
ISBN-10: 0-545-06927-0

Publisher: Dominic Carman
Art director: Ivo Marloh
Managing editor: Paul Docherty
Project editor: Deborah Hercun
Design: Claire Harvey
Layout: 3rd-I
Production: Nikki Ingram
Picture research: Veneta Bullen

Printed and bound in China by SNP Leefung Printers Ltd.

10 9 8 7 6 5 4 3

First printing, October 2008

Anna Claybourne

100 MOST DANGEROUS THINGS ON THE PLANET

CONTENTS

Human Dangers

INTRODUCTION

Today the world is probably safer for humans than it has ever been. Modern medicines, emergency services, warm dry houses, and clean water supplies have saved millions of lives. That's why, in most countries, the population is rising, and people are living longer and longer.

WILD WORLD

However, there are still some dangers that we can do little about. Human technology is no match for the mighty power of an exploding volcano or the force of a 100-foot- (30-m) high tsunami, or a powerful tornado. And much of our world is made up of remote wilderness and ocean, where you can easily get lost, or find yourself face-to-face with a dangerous animal.

LOOK AFTER YOURSELF

Of course, the best way to stay safe is to avoid dangerous situations in the first place.

STAY AWAY

Don't explore wild places alone, or without the right equipment. Whenever you can, keep clear of the kinds of dangerous things described in this book, such as thin ice, poisonous animals, or avalanche-risk areas.

WARNING

This book contains the most useful advice available for various dangerous situations. But the tips here are only general guidelines, and cannot be guaranteed to keep you safe. In a dangerous situation, there may be no truly safe option.

USE COMMON SENSE
Never do dangerous things for a laugh or a dare. If you don't feel safe, or you know something is risky, don't do it. If other people are doing it, try to persuade them not to, or get help.

HEED WARNINGS
In many dangerous places, such as crumbling cliffs and beaches with strong currents, there are signs to warn you where it's not safe to go. They are there to help you—don't ignore them!

OBEY INSTRUCTIONS
This book contains useful tips for lots of different kinds of dangers. But in a *particular* situation, such as an earthquake in your area, or seeing a dangerous animal, you should follow any instructions given to you by local guides, emergency services, or local warning systems. They are more likely to know the best course of action for that particular event.

On February 22, 1999, two large avalanches hit the town of Evolene in the Swiss Alps. Twelve people were killed, and more than a dozen went missing.

RISK RATING

☠	Rare
☠ ☠	Unlikely
☠ ☠ ☠	Likely
☠ ☠ ☠ ☠	Very Likely
☠ ☠ ☠ ☠ ☠	Frequent

DID YOU KNOW?
- A lightning bolt can be 6 times hotter than the surface of the Sun
- Hippos kill far more people than sharks do
- One of the biggest dangers in deserts is the cold—the temperature can be freezing at night

READ ON TO FIND OUT MORE...

NATURAL

Much of our planet is wild and full of natural dangers. You could get lost in one of the world's vast deserts, jungles, oceans, or icy polar regions, or you could encounter a dangerous animal such as

DANGERS

a deadly snake, spider, or jellyfish. Natural disasters such as earthquakes and tsunamis, and violent weather such as tornadoes and lightning, can affect us even when we're at home.

VOLCANIC ERUPTION

When a volcano erupts, hot lava (melted rock), gas, and burning ash burst out from inside Earth. An eruption can fling solid rock into the air, too. Most volcanoes have erupted many times before, forming mountains. They are closely monitored, so if one is about to erupt, there will usually be lots of warnings. But people do sometimes get caught in an eruption.

WHAT TO DO

IF THERE'S A WARNING:
The local area will be evacuated. Follow instructions and leave the area as quickly and safely as possible. Take blankets, food, and water in case you get stuck.

IF A VOLCANO ERUPTS NEAR YOU:
Head for high ground to avoid lava and mud that may flow down valleys. Wear clothes that protect you from falling ash. Protect your eyes with goggles, and your mouth and nose with a wet facecloth.

IF A VOLCANO ERUPTS WHILE YOU'RE ON IT:
Head for a high ridge on the mountainside and avoid valleys, streams, and bridges. Look for large rocks for shelter.

DANGER RATING

RISK RATING: ☠ ☠ ☠
Millions of people live close to volcanoes, but there are only around 60 eruptions a year.

SURVIVAL RATING: 80%
You should be able to escape, even if you're on the volcano.

TOP TIP! If rocks start falling around you, curl up and cover your head!

LAVA FLOW

Some volcanoes erupt very gently and quietly. There's no big explosion—just lava flowing down the volcano's sides. It could take you by surprise if it suddenly flows faster or changes direction.

You can even have a lava flow without a volcano. Sometimes lava comes to the surface of Earth's crust in an unexpected place, forming a new volcano.

WHAT TO DO

IF A LAVA FLOW IS COMING:

If you see lava heading your way, move quickly, heading uphill. Check for other lava flows as you go, so that you don't get trapped. Steer clear of water and plants, as lava can explode when it touches them.

IF LAVA SURROUNDS YOU:

You need to get away fast, while

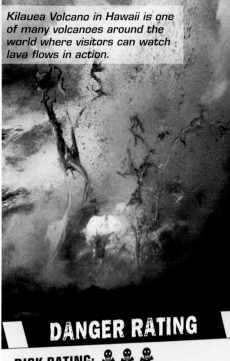

Kilauea Volcano in Hawaii is one of many volcanoes around the world where visitors can watch lava flows in action.

DANGER RATING

RISK RATING: ☠ ☠ ☠
Lava is a danger to the many tourists who visit active volcanoes.

SURVIVAL RATING: 90%
As most lava is slow-moving, you can usually get away from it.

the flow is small. Jump over it if you can do so safely. Or look out for rocks you can use as stepping stones. Avoid stepping on fresh lava, even if it looks solid.

AVOID LAVA BURNS:

Near lava, wear tough leather boots, long sleeves and pants, a hat, gloves, and sunglasses or goggles. If lava spatters or explodes, turn your face away quickly to avoid burns.

HOW HOT?

Lava is VERY HOT. It is made of melted rock—and it takes very high temperatures to melt rock. Most lava is at least 930°F (500°C), but it can be as hot as 2,370°F (1,300°C).

PYROCLASTIC FLOW

A pyroclastic flow is one of the most dangerous and deadly of all volcanic events. It is a mixture of hot gas, rocks, and ash that surges downhill from an erupting volcano. It moves fast, like a flowing river. In fact, pyroclastic flows can reach speeds of 100 mph (160 kph) and can be as hot as 1,300°F (700°C). You do NOT want to be caught up in one!

WHAT TO DO

IF A PYROCLASTIC FLOW IS COMING:

You can't move fast enough to outrun a pyroclastic flow, even in a car. Instead, try to see where it's headed and get out of the way. Head to the side and away from low ground.

IF YOU'RE IN THE WAY:

If a pyroclastic flow lands on you, it's too late! But if you're near the edge of the flow, you could survive. Hide behind a rock, or in any shelter you can find, such as a hut. As the flow passes, cover your head and hold your breath. Breathing in the hot gas, dust, and ash can destroy your lungs.

DANGER RATING

RISK RATING: ☠
Pyroclastic flows are very rare, occuring only a few times a year.

SURVIVAL RATING: 10%
Your only chance of survival is to avoid the path of the flow.

DID YOU KNOW?

The ancient Italian town of Pompeii was flattened by a pyroclastic flow from the volcano Vesuvius in AD 79. The ash hardened around the victims' bodies, forming human-shaped spaces.

MUDFLOW OR LAHAR

A volcanic mudflow, or lahar, happens when volcanic ash mixes with water. The water can come from heavy rain, from a lake or river, or a volcanic eruption melting snow and ice. The mixture forms fast-flowing mud that can rush down a volcano's valleys and drown whole towns. Like a river, a lahar can travel a long way from the eruption itself.

WHAT TO DO

IF THERE'S A WARNING:
Many areas at risk of mudflows have warning systems in place. Obey the instructions and move away from valleys and rivers to high ground as fast as you can.

IF A MUDFLOW STRIKES:
If you're caught in a lahar, you'll be safer the higher up you are. Go inside a tall, strong building and go upstairs. If there's no building, climbing a large tree could save your life.

TRAPPED IN THE MUD:
Try to keep your head above the mud and cling on to floating objects as you wait for rescue.

DANGER RATING

RISK RATING: ☠ ☠
There's almost always a risk of mudflows when a volcano erupts.

SURVIVAL RATING: 90%
Mudflows have been big killers in the past, but today's satellite technology can usually see them coming.

MUDFLOW HORROR

In 1985, a lahar from the Nevado del Ruiz volcano in Colombia drowned the town of Armero, killing over 23,000 people. If they had known it was coming, the townspeople could have climbed to nearby high ground and escaped.

SUPERVOLCANO

A supervolcano is a huge volcanic eruption, far bigger than a normal volcano. As a normal volcano erupts, lava cools and builds up around it, making a mountain. But a supervolcano throws so much lava and rock out of the ground that it leaves a bowl-shaped crater, or caldera.

There were several supervolcanic eruptions in prehistoric times. For example, Yellowstone National Park in the U.S.A. is on the site of an old supervolcano, which might one day erupt again.

WHAT TO DO

IF A SUPERVOLCANO IS PREDICTED:

If there's time, the area around the supervolcano will be evacuated. Leave quickly, but stay calm to avoid travel chaos.

DURING THE ERUPTION:

If you're more than 60 miles (100 km) from the eruption, you could survive. A heavy ash fall will cover the land for thousands of miles in every direction. Stay indoors to shelter from it—don't try to drive through it.

AFTER THE EVENT:

Ash thrown into orbit will surround Earth and blot out sunlight, making it hard to grow crops. You may be able to survive on stockpiled, preserved foods.

DANGER RATING

RISK RATING: ☠

A supervolcano will erupt again, but maybe not for a long time.

SURVIVAL RATING: 50%

A big supervolcano would destroy a huge area, and many people would die.

TOP TIP! Don't panic! There's so little we can do about a supervolcano, there's no point worrying about it.

AVALANCHE

An avalanche happens when a big pile of snow slips down a mountainside. Many things can cause avalanches—wind, sunshine melting the snow, snowmobiles or skiers dislodging it, or new snow piling up into an unstable heap.

Avalanches can be deadly if the snow buries people or houses. It is heavy and hard to dig through, and people often run out of air before rescuers can reach them.

DANGER RATING

RISK RATING: ☠ ☠ ☠
Avalanches happen every year, often in popular ski resorts.

SURVIVAL RATING: 60%
You can survive if you can avoid the path of the avalanche or dig your way out.

HI-TECH HELP
Many skiers now carry an avalanche transceiver. This gadget gives out a radio signal that lets rescuers locate them if they are buried by an avalanche.

WHAT TO DO

IF YOU SEE AN AVALANCHE:
Move sideways to try to avoid the avalanche. Try to take shelter behind a large rock or hold on to a tree and try to stay upright.

IF YOU'RE SWEPT AWAY:
Drop your backpack, as it will weigh you down. Make swimming movements to try to stay on the surface of the snow.

IF YOU'RE BURIED IN THE SNOW:
Curl into a ball, with your hands in front of your face to make a space for air. Spit into your hands—the spit will fall downward, so you know the other way is up. Dig upward with your hands or a ski pole before the snow hardens.

EARTHQUAKE

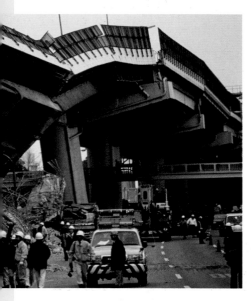

Earth's crust (surface layer) is made up of several large sections, called tectonic plates. They slowly move around, squeezing and grinding against one another. Sometimes, they catch one another, and the tension builds up until the plates suddenly slip. The ground jerks and trembles in an earthquake. Big earthquakes can tear cracks in the ground, causing buildings to collapse.

During a massive earthquake in 1995 a freeway collapsed in Kobe, Japan.

WHAT TO DO

EARTHQUAKE WARNING:

It's hard for scientists to predict earthquakes, but they sometimes can. It may be possible to evacuate the area in time. If an earthquake is coming, prepare. Put heavy objects on the floor. Collect plenty of water in buckets and bottles. Put out any fires and flames safely.

DURING AN EARTHQUAKE:

If you're indoors, shelter in a doorway or under a heavy table or desk. Stay away from the kitchen, stairways, elevators, and windows. If you're outdoors, move away from houses, trees, power lines, bridges, and other things that could fall on you.

DANGER RATING

RISK RATING: ☠ ☠ ☠
There are dozens of major earthquakes around the world each year.

SURVIVAL RATING: 80%
Earthquakes can be disastrous, but in most cases, many people survive.

TOP TIP! After an earthquake, there could be another quake, or smaller shakes called tremors. Don't assume the quake is over—avoid danger while you wait for rescue.

DANGER RATING

RISK RATING: ☠ ☠

A sinkhole opening under your house or street is very unlikely.

SURVIVAL RATING: 60%

You may survive falling into a sinkhole, or be able to run away before you do.

This sinkhole appeared in Guatemala City, Guatemala, in 2007. It swallowed up 12 houses and killed three people.

SINKHOLE

Imagine a huge hole in the ground suddenly opening up right under your feet! A sinkhole is simply a hole in the ground, caused by water wearing away underground rocks. Many sinkholes form gradually. But sometimes, water hollows out an invisible underground chamber, covered by a thin layer of rock. Eventually this "roof" collapses inward, and a gaping hole appears. If this happens in a busy built-up area, it can be disastrous.

WHAT TO DO

SPOT A SINKHOLE:

Sinkholes can appear without warning. Sometimes, though, there are warning signs, such as a circular pattern of cracks in the ground, earth tremors, and a deep rumbling noise. If these things happen, leave the area and call the emergency services.

IF A SINKHOLE APPEARS:

If the ground starts to sink, run uphill toward the edge of the sinkhole. Hold on to railings or other fixed objects to pull yourself up.

IF YOU FALL IN:

You might land in water, which will break your fall. Tread water, cling to floating objects, and yell!

DID YOU KNOW?

Sometimes, a sinkhole opens up at the bottom of a lake. The lake disappears into it, like bath water going down the drain.

TSUNAMI

Tourists and locals run for their lives from the massive Indian Ocean tsunami of 2004.

A tsunami is a giant wave or series of waves that crash onto the shore, usually because of an undersea earthquake. As a tsunami nears the shore, it builds up into a wall of water, which can reach heights of 30 to 100 feet (10–30 m). The force of the water can destroy everything in its path.

DANGER RATING

RISK RATING: ☠ ☠ ☠

There are several large tsunamis each year around the world. Being caught in one is unlikely, but when they strike they can kill thousands.

SURVIVAL RATING: 70%

If a tsunami strikes a town or village, it will almost certainly be a killer. But you have a good chance of survival if you know what to do.

WHAT TO DO

IF A TSUNAMI IS COMING:
Head inland as fast as you can and aim for high ground. Try to get to the top of a tall hill. Alternatively, go inside the biggest, strongest building you can see and make for an upper floor.

IF THE WAVE IS ABOUT TO HIT YOU:
Climb a tree or grab hold of a fixed object such as a railing or parking meter. Use your clothes to tie yourself to it, and try to cling on as the tsunami passes.

IF IT WASHES YOU AWAY:
Look for a floating object to hold on to, and try to protect your head. Yell for help.

WARNING SIGNS:
These signs can sometimes tell you a tsunami is on the way:
• You feel an earthquake when you're close to the shore.
• The sea suddenly becomes rough and boats bob up and down.
• The sea is quickly sucked away from the beach, leaving the seabed bare.

TOP TIP! Some areas, especially around the Pacific where tsunamis are most common, have signs showing you where to go if one is coming.

TSUNAMI HAZARD ZONE

IN CASE OF EARTHQUAKE
TO HIGH GROUND OR INL

ASTEROID STRIKE

DANGER RATING

An asteroid is a lump of rock zooming through space. Most are far away from Earth, but sometimes one comes so close to Earth that gravity sucks it in, and it falls to the ground.

A big asteroid strike could have devastating results. It would flatten the area it landed on, blow out a huge crater, and trigger tsunamis. It could also fill the sky with debris, blocking out the sunlight.

WHAT TO DO

IF AN ASTEROID IS COMING:

Scientists should be able to predict a strike, giving time to warn the public. The likely landing site would be evacuated. It would be wise to stockpile food and water. People on the coast should head for high ground, in case of tsunamis.

IF IT'S ABOUT TO LAND:

If an asteroid hits you, you'll have no chance. But if it's far away, you could survive. Shelter from the initial blast under doorways or heavy furniture.

AFTER THE IMPACT:

Stay indoors to hide from falling debris. Later, you may be able to travel to a safer area.

RISK RATING: ☠
The chance of an asteroid landing on you is tiny.

SURVIVAL RATING: 50%
It depends on the asteroid—a small one might not harm anyone, but a big one could wipe out life on Earth.

Asteroids range from pea-sized to many miles wide. An asteroid 33 feet (10 m) across could destroy a town. An asteroid 330 feet (100 m) across could destroy an area the size of Britain. An asteroid 6 miles (10 km) across could wipe out the human race.

DID YOU KNOW? Scientists are working on ways to deflect asteroids that come too close. One idea is firing a rocket at an asteroid to make it change direction and miss Earth.

FREAK WAVE

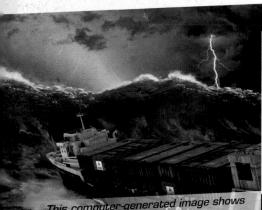

This computer-generated image shows the awesome scale of a freak wave.

DANGER RATING

RISK RATING: ☠
Freak waves are rare, and it's even rarer that they hit a boat.
SURVIVAL RATING: 70%
If the wave doesn't sink your boat in seconds, you'll probably escape its worst effects.

A freak, or rogue, wave is a giant wave that appears far out at sea. It is not a tsunami or a storm wave. It's just a sea wave that is much, much bigger and steeper than normal. The biggest storm waves are about 50 feet (15 m) high, but a freak wave can reach 80 feet (25 m) or even 100 feet (30 m) high. Freak waves may lie behind many unexplained sinkings.

Experts think freak waves can be caused by wind, currents, or by several waves joining together, but they are not sure.

DID YOU KNOW?

Sailors have been reporting freak waves for centuries, but many people thought they were just exaggerated tales. In 2003, scientists proved freak waves existed by using satellites in space to detect them.

WHAT TO DO

IF YOU SEE A FREAK WAVE:
If you're on a ship and you see a freak wave, get indoors fast. Move to the other side of the ship, away from the wave. Stay away from windows. Find something to hold on to and hang on tight.

IF THE WAVE CRASHES OVER YOU:
If you're on deck when the wave comes, your only chance is to grab something fixed, such as a railing, and hang on to it. Put your head down and hold your breath as the wave passes.

AVOIDING FREAK WAVES:
Scientists are trying to calculate where in the world freak waves happen most, and working on early warning systems to help boats avoid freak wave disasters.

ICEBERG

The word "iceberg" means "ice mountain." An iceberg is a huge, floating chunk of ice that has broken off from a glacier. Icebergs form around the Arctic and Antarctic, where glaciers (slow rivers of ice) flow into the sea and break up.

Ice is slightly lighter than water. This means that icebergs float—but only just. As an iceberg drifts, only about 12 percent is visible above the surface; the rest is underwater. The rock-hard ice can cause disaster if a ship hits it.

WHAT TO DO

IF YOU SEE AN ICEBERG:
All kinds of boats should stay away from icebergs. Even if it looks far away, part of the iceberg could be just under the water nearby. Never go closer to get a better look. Icebergs can suddenly roll over or shed big lumps of ice, creating dangerous waves.

IF YOU HIT AN ICEBERG:
An iceberg can rip a boat open under the waterline. If you're on a big ship, such as a cruiser, go to an upper deck and follow any instructions from the captain and crew.

This cross section picture shows how much of an iceberg is underwater.

DANGER RATING

RISK RATING: ☠ ☠ ☠
There are thousands of icebergs floating around. They are a constant danger to ships, undersea cables, and oil rigs.

SURVIVAL RATING: 80%
As icebergs move slowly, it's usually possible to avoid them.

THE TITANIC

An iceberg caused one of the most famous disasters in history—the sinking of the Titanic in 1912. People said the new ocean liner was unsinkable, but she hit an iceberg and sank within hours. There were not enough lifeboats, and around 1,500 people died.

FLOOD

A flood happens when water overflows an area of land. Many rivers flood the land around them every year without causing problems, because people know what to expect. But sudden, unexpected flooding can be much more serious. It can be caused by heavy rainfall, or by the sea overflowing the land because of a sea storm or tsunami.

Floodwater can sweep away people, cars, and houses, or cause damage by spreading mud and sewage far and wide.

A man wearing garbage bags on his legs struggles through the floodwaters in Venice.

WHAT TO DO

IF THERE'S A FLOOD WARNING:

Leave the area and go stay somewhere safer. Make sure pets are safe, too. Move valuable and electrical items upstairs or put them high up. Switch off the gas and electricity supply, and if you have them, pile sandbags around your home. If you are staying, store fresh water, food, a first aid kit, flashlights, and blankets.

IF YOU'RE CUT OFF BY FLOODWATER:

Stay calm! Try to contact the emergency services using a cell phone if possible. Otherwise, wave

DANGER RATING

RISK RATING: ☠ ☠ ☠ ☠
Floods happen all around the world every year, and they are becoming more common.

SURVIVAL RATING: 90%
Though floods can be very dangerous, they usually cause more damage to property than to people.

or shine a flashlight at passing boats or helicopters. Keep any food and water supplies safe. Don't try to escape through the water—wait to be rescued.

IF YOU'RE SWEPT AWAY:

Cling to floating objects and try to grab on to a tree or signpost. Yell and wave to help rescuers see you.

FLASH FLOOD

Hurricane Dean caused severe flash floods in August 2007 in Dominica.

Flash floods are floods that occur suddenly. Usually, a flash flood is caused by a thunderstorm dropping a lot of heavy rain in a short time. It can collect into a torrent of water that surges down narrow river valleys. A dam collapsing can also cause a flash flood.

Flash floods are dangerous because they take people by surprise. They often happen in summer, when rivers are calm and people are enjoying fishing, hiking, or swimming there.

DANGER RATING

RISK RATING: ☠ ☠
Flash floods are much rarer than other types of flood.
SURVIVAL RATING: 60%
Flash floods move so fast that it can be difficult to get away.

WHAT TO DO

IF YOU SEE OR HEAR A FLASH FLOOD COMING:
If you're in a valley, you may spot a flash flood upriver, or hear a loud roaring sound. Move fast—climb up the sides of the valley, away from the water. As the flood approaches, look for a tree to hold on to.

IF YOU'RE SWEPT AWAY:
Try to tread water or hold on to a floating branch, and swim for the bank. If you can, grab a tree on the bank and hold on.

AVOID FLASH FLOODS:
Flash floods are hard to predict, but think twice before visiting a deep valley or gorge if you know heavy rain is in the forecast.

DID YOU KNOW?
Many of the victims of flash floods die not from drowning, but from being hit by the rocks, branches, and logs carried along by the powerful surging water.

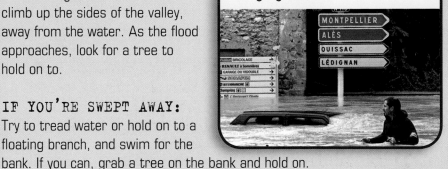

LANDSLIDE

In June 2005 a massive landslide in Laguna Beach, California, sent 18 homes crashing down a hill.

A landslide is just what it sounds like—a section of land sliding downhill. They can happen on steep slopes or cliffs when the ground is soaked by heavy rain or melting snow, making the soil heavy and slippery. Earthquakes and volcanic eruptions can also trigger landslides. A landslide can cause a disaster if the rock and soil fall on houses, or if it falls into water, causing a tsunami.

DANGER RATING

RISK RATING: ☠ ☠ ☠
Landslides are fairly common, though most are quite small.

SURVIVAL RATING: 80%
Most landslides don't fall on people, and even when they do, some survive.

WHAT TO DO

LOOK OUT FOR LANDSLIDES:

You can sometimes tell that a landslide is about to happen. You might see small trickles of soil flowing downhill, and trees might start to tilt as the earth shifts. Stream water may turn muddy. If you see these signs, call the emergency services and leave the area, warning neighbors, too.

DURING A LANDSLIDE:

If there's time, head sideways out of the path of the landslide. Don't try to take anything with you—drop everything and run. If the landslide is going to fall on you, curl into a ball with your arms around your head. If you're indoors, shelter under heavy furniture. Outdoors, hide behind a big rock or tree.

DAM DISASTER In 1963, a landslide plunged into a reservoir behind the Vaiont Dam in Italy. It created a huge wave, which flowed over the dam and onto several villages below, killing 2,000 people.

SOLAR FLARE

Our sun is a giant ball of very hot, burning gas. On its surface are cooler areas known as sunspots. Sometimes, near a sunspot, a massive explosion of energy bursts out from the sun. This is a solar flare. It flings out huge amounts of radiation, such as X-rays, into space. If these rays are thrown toward Earth, they can damage electronic equipment, such as space satellites. If a really big solar flare hit Earth, experts think it might destroy electrical systems and cause a major disaster.

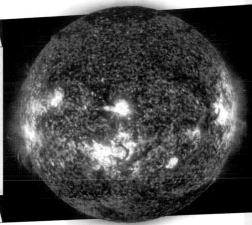

DANGER RATING

RISK RATING: ☠
Solar flares happen regularly, but one big enough to cause disaster is not very likely.

SURVIVAL RATING: 50%
A really huge solar flare could lead to devastation on Earth.

WHAT TO DO

DON'T WORRY:
We can't control the sun, so there's nothing we can do to stop a massive solar flare. And if it affects the whole Earth, there's nowhere to escape to anyway. It is also very unlikely.

IF IT HAPPENS:
A giant solar flare might cut off electricity and communications systems. This would bring the world to a standstill—things like banks, transport systems, GPS networks, phones, and computers would stop working. The best preparation for this is to have good basic survival skills and equipment, such as flashlights, tools, and first aid knowledge.

DID YOU KNOW? Sunspots and solar flares follow a regular cycle. Every 11 years or so, they reach maximum strength, then calm down again. The next peak is due around 2011.

LAKE OVERTURN

When you open a fizzy drink bottle, bubbles zoom up to the top. The same thing can happen in a lake. Some lakes form over volcanic vents, which release gases into the water. If the lake is deep, the water at the bottom is under great pressure. The gas dissolves in the deep water, and the water above holds it down.

But if something disturbs the lake, such as an earth tremor, the gas-filled water can rise to the surface. The gas escapes in what is known as a limnic eruption, or a lake overturn. It rolls out of the lake in a huge cloud that can suffocate people and animals.

WHAT TO DO

IF YOU SEE BUBBLES FORMING:

If you see lake water starting to fizz and bubble, it could be the start of a lake overturn. Head uphill from the lake and raise the alarm.

IF YOU'RE CAUGHT IN A GAS CLOUD:

The gas in a lake overturn is usually carbon dioxide. It is heavier than air, so it flows downhill into valleys. To escape, move uphill, away from valleys and low areas.

PREVENTING LAKE OVERTURNS:

Scientists are trying to prevent lake overturns by installing pipes in some volcanic lakes. The pipe lets gas escape from the depths of the lake at a slow, safe rate.

DANGER RATING

RISK RATING:
There are only a handful of lake overturns on record.

SURVIVAL RATING: 30%
When they happen, lake overturns are very dangerous.

LAKE NYOS The deadliest lake overturn on record happened at Lake Nyos in Cameroon, Africa, in 1986. It killed about 1,700 people and thousands of cattle.

SEICHE

"Seiche" is a French word that means "sway." During a seiche, the water in a lake, bay, or pond sways or sloshes to and fro. First it rises up at one end of the lake, and down at the other. Then it sloshes back the other way. As the water rocks back and forth, it can overflow onto the land, sweeping people away and causing floods.

Seiches are usually caused by storms and strong winds pushing at the lake surface. Earthquakes and volcanic eruptions can sometimes cause seiches, too.

WHAT TO DO

SEICHE WARNING:
On lakes that have regular seiches, such as Lake Michigan in the U.S.A., there are warnings when a seiche is likely. Avoid the lakeshore, don't go out in a boat, and keep away from piers.

DURING A SEICHE:
In a seiche, water can rise up suddenly and wash over the shore. If you see it coming, run inland or get inside a building. If you are washed away, stay calm. Try to swim toward the shore and cling on to railings, a tree, or other fixed object until the water subsides.

The Great Lakes of Canada and the U.S.A. have seiches, known locally as sloshes, on a regular basis. Lake Erie is particularly affected because of its long shape and shallow water.

DANGER RATING

RISK RATING: ☠ ☠
Seiches are fairly rare, and most of them are quite small.

SURVIVAL RATING: 90%
Seiches can be killers, but there is usually a warning. Most seiches are not big like tsunamis.

A seiche works just like water sloshing to and fro in a bathtub.

DID YOU KNOW?
Seiches can happen in swimming pools—especially after an earthquake. If you're swimming when an earthquake happens, get out of the water.

WILDFIRE

When fire sweeps through forests, fields, or outback, it's called a wildfire. Most wildfires happen in summer and fall, when trees and grass have dried out and catch fire easily. Wind can fan the flames and help the fire spread. Wildfires destroy thousands of trees and plants. Sometimes, they burn down houses or trap people in their cars.

Some wildfires start naturally, sparked by lightning or a volcanic eruption. Others are caused by people making campfires, dropping cigarettes, or even starting a fire on purpose to cause damage.

DANGER RATING

RISK RATING: ☠ ☠ ☠
Wildfires are a serious danger in many parts of the world, and hundreds happen every year.

SURVIVAL RATING: 80%
Being caught in a wildfire is very dangerous, but people usually manage to get away.

WHAT TO DO

IF THERE'S A WILDFIRE WARNING:

Check radio and T.V. broadcasts for evacuation instructions. Plan an escape route and talk to your neighbors—if your family has a car, you could arrange to take someone who doesn't. Find your pets and have them ready to go. Put important documents and emergency supplies in the car, which should be ready with the keys in the ignition.

IF A WILDFIRE IS CLOSING IN:

If you're at home, use a hose to wet the roof, walls, and surroundings. If you're on the move, check the direction of the smoke and flames to see where the fire is going, and head another way. If the fire is about to catch you, you'll be safest in water. Look for a river or lake that you can get into safely.

TOP TIP! You can help to prevent wildfires. Don't start campfires in the wild, and always take all your litter home with you.

FIRESTORM

A firestorm is a very intense, dangerous kind of wildfire that creates a fiery windstorm. As a fire burns, it causes an updraft. The hot air rises upward, and cooler air is sucked inward to replace it. If the fire is very intense, this effect can create powerful whirlwinds and even lightning. In turn, the winds fan the flames, making the fire far hotter than a normal wildfire. As well as spreading the fire, firestorm winds fill the air with smoke, making it hard to see.

WHAT TO DO

SPOT A FIRESTORM:

Signs of a firestorm include the noise of the fire getting quieter at first, then much louder. You may see a mushroom-shaped cloud of smoke above the fire, and feel the air getting very hot, even from some distance away.

In the summer of 2007, fires raged across large parts of Greece. Here a firefighting airplane battles a firestorm in the forest of Mount Hymettus, on the edge of Athens.

GET AWAY:

If you see a firestorm, don't stick around. Move away from it quickly, in a car if possible. Don't stop to stare at it!

IF YOU ARE TRAPPED:

If the firestorm is on top of you, your only chance is to get into water, or get down as low as you can. Inside a house, shut yourself in the basement. In a forest, try to crawl away from the fire, covering your face with your clothes.

DID YOU KNOW?

Firestorms can also happen during fires in cities. The Great Fire of London, which destroyed most of the city in 1666, is thought to have involved a firestorm.

HURRICANE

Hurricane Georges battering the coast of Puerto Rico in September 1998.

DANGER RATING

RISK RATING: 💀 💀 💀 💀
Big hurricanes happen every year, and experts think they are becoming more common as Earth gets warmer.

SURVIVAL RATING: 90%
Hurricanes can be deadly, but as there's plenty of warning, most people survive.

Hurricanes are the world's biggest storms. They form over the ocean, when warm weather makes hot, damp air rise upward. This sucks in more air, which spins around and around, building a giant spiral of swirling rain clouds.

A hurricane can be 300 miles (500 km) across, with wind speeds of up to 180 mph (290 kph). Usually, hurricanes move slowly across the sea until they meet land. There they can cause great devastation.

WHAT TO DO

WHEN A HURRICANE COMES:
Scientists can track hurricanes at sea using satellites, so they usually know when one is coming. If you are told to evacuate the area, fill your car with gas, pack emergency food, water, medicines, and blankets, and head inland. If there's time, protect your home. Move all outdoor furniture and objects inside. If you don't have window shutters, fix plywood boards over the windows.

DURING A HURRICANE:
You'll be safest indoors. Stay in the middle of the building you are in, away from windows. If you're outdoors, look for any kind of shelter. Don't hide under a bridge, though, as the wind may speed up there. Keep away from floodwater, and avoid power lines as they could fall on you.

TOP TIP! If the weather suddenly goes calm and quiet, don't think it's all over! It's probably just the "eye" of the hurricane—the small calm area in the middle of the storm. Stay where you are until the rest of the hurricane has passed by.

TORNADO

A tornado is smaller than a hurricane, but its winds can be even faster—up to 300 mph (500 kph). Tornadoes form during thunderstorms, when a column of air moves downward from a thundercloud. More air spirals around it, forming a cone-shaped funnel of wind. Most tornadoes look dark because their strong winds pick up dust, rubble, and debris. Tornadoes can cause devastation, flattening homes and flinging cars around as they track across the land.

WHAT TO DO

IF A TORNADO IS COMING:

If you spot a tornado, get indoors and hide in a basement, or in a downstairs room in the middle of the house. Shelter under a heavy table and put cushions or blankets around it to catch flying objects. Mobile homes are not safe. If you're in one, leave it and shelter in a solid building, or a purpose-built tornado shelter.

SKY SIGN You can sometimes tell when a tornado is about to form, because the sky turns a strange dark green color!

IF YOU'RE OUTDOORS:

If you're in a car, get out of it and run for shelter. Tornadoes can lift cars high into the air, then drop them. If there's no building to shelter in, lie down in a ditch and cover your head.

A killer tornado tears up southern Maryland in April 2002. Wind speeds reached up to 318 mph (509 kph), killing two people and injuring 95 in the devastated town of La Plata.

BLIZZARD

A blizzard is a severe snowstorm in which heavy snowfall combines with swirling winds. The snow whirls around and fills the air, making it very hard to see where you are going. Meanwhile, snowdrifts collect on the ground, making driving and walking almost impossible. Being caught outdoors in a blizzard is very dangerous.

WHAT TO DO

IN BLIZZARD CONDITIONS: Stay at home, or shelter in a shop or another warm building as soon as you can. It's a good idea to leave some lights on in case someone else is lost in the blizzard and searching for shelter.

IF YOU'RE IN A CAR: Make sure the car is pulled over in a safe place as soon as possible. Call for help using a cell phone, and switch on the lights to help emergency services find you. While you're waiting, wrap up in coats, hats, blankets, and any other coverings you can find.

IF YOU'RE ON FOOT: Call for help on a cell phone if possible. Look out for lights that could show you where a house is, or use any kind of shelter you can find, like a bus shelter, cave, or phone booth. Wear all the clothes you have with you, and keep your hands and head covered to ward off frostbite.

A snow plow lies crashed in Slovakia after the region was hit by heavy snowstorms in 2005.

FROSTBITE

Frostbite is a danger in snow and ice storms. It happens when blood vessels freeze in a body part such as your fingers, toes, or nose. The affected part goes black, and may have to be cut off.

ICE STORM

DANGER RATING

RISK RATING: ☠ ☠ ☠
Ice storms mainly happen in the
U.S.A. and Canada. A bad one
comes along every few years.

SURVIVAL RATING: 95%
Usually, most of the people
caught in an ice storm survive.

A severe ice storm in 1998 in eastern Canada and upstate New York caused 4 million people to lose power, some for weeks.

An ice storm may sound wild and violent, but ice storms can actually be quite peaceful. However, they are still dangerous! They occur when very cold rain falls in freezing cold weather. The rain is liquid, but as soon as it lands on icy cold roads, houses, and trees, it freezes solid. Over time, a layer of very thick, heavy, slippery ice builds up. As well as causing skidding accidents on roads, ice can weigh down tree branches, roofs, and power lines until they snap.

WHAT TO DO

WHEN AN ICE STORM STRIKES:
If possible, stay indoors. Falling ice, tree branches, and power lines can be deadly. Driving in an ice storm is a bad idea, as roads are slippery and can be blocked by fallen trees.

IF YOU'RE CUT OFF:
Ice storms can cut off electricity and communications cables, leaving you isolated. Stay in and wait for the emergency services to check your home.

COMBAT THE COLD:
If you're cut off with no heating, try to keep warm. Everyone in the house should gather in one room with blankets, duvets, hats, and gloves. If you have a coal or wood fire, or stove with a proper flue or chimney, keep it lit and huddle around it.

TOP TIP! Never, ever bring a barbecue or other outdoor fire device indoors to keep you warm. They can give off poisonous fumes and have killed several people in past ice storms.

HAILSTORM

Hail is made up of hailstones—hard balls of ice that fall from the clouds. Hail forms inside thunderclouds. Each hailstone starts as a tiny object, such as a speck of dust, a small seed, or even a small insect. As strong winds blow it around inside the cloud, it bumps into icy cold raindrops. They freeze solid around it, building up layers of ice. When the hailstone is heavy enough, it falls. Ice is heavy, so even small hailstones can cause a lot of damage. And sometimes, giant hailstones fall in terrifying torrents.

HUGE HAILSTONE

Hailstones can be small as peas, or as big as golf balls. The biggest hailstone on record fell on Aurora, Nebraska, U.S.A. in 2003. It measured an incredible 7 inches (18 cm) across.

DANGER RATING

RISK RATING: ☠ ☠ ☠ ☠
Most parts of the world experience hail several times a year.

SURVIVAL RATING: 95%
Hail can be deadly, but generally only if the hailstones are unusually large.

WHAT TO DO

IF THERE'S A RISK OF HAIL:

It's hard to predict a hailstorm, but hail happens most often during thunderstorms. So if thunderstorms are in the forecast, avoid going out into remote areas or doing outdoor activities.

DURING A HAILSTORM:

Stay indoors and keep away from windows, as the hail could break a window and shower you with glass. If you're out and about, and the hail is so heavy it seems dangerous, shelter under a doorway, a park bench, or even a parked car. If you're in a moving car, you should stop somewhere safe and huddle into the middle of the vehicle, away from the windows. Take care, as hail can make the ground slippery.

FROG FALL

Can it really rain frogs? The answer is yes, and it can also rain toads, fish, birds, jellyfish, and various other animals! These mysterious "falls" are very rare, but they have been reported around the world. Experts think that sometimes a waterspout—a kind of tornado over water—sucks up sea or lake animals and carries them over land, where they fall back down. Flocks of birds may fall like rain after flying into violent stormclouds.

DANGER RATING

RISK RATING: ☠
Showers of animals are pretty rare—and it's even less likely that one will fall on you.

SURVIVAL RATING: 95%
Animal falls have not claimed many lives—but a falling animal could be dangerous if it hits you.

WHAT TO DO

IF IT RAINS ANIMALS:

These events are very rare and cannot be predicted. If you suddenly find frogs, fish, or other animals falling around you, head for shelter immediately. The danger is that you will be so amazed or fascinated, you'll forget to run for cover! But even a small frog or fish falling from a great height could seriously injure you.

AFTER THE SHOWER:

When the weird weather has cleared, you might be tempted to go and examine the animals. Take care—animals have been known to survive the fall, and they may bite or sting.

DID YOU KNOW?

Animal showers have been happening for thousands of years. Frog and fish falls were reported in medieval times and in ancient Greece.

SANDSTORM

Sandstorms occur when a strong wind picks up a lot of sand and carries it through the air. The same thing can happen with dust during a drought.

Sandstorms and dust storms are dangerous because they fill the air with particles, making it hard to see and breathe. They can cause car and airplane accidents, and damage homes by dumping heavy sand on them.

DANGER RATING

RISK RATING: ☠ ☠ ☠
Sandstorms and dust storms are a common risk in dry areas.

SURVIVAL RATING: 90%
You're very likely to survive a sandstorm, especially if you have a car or building to shelter in.

WHAT TO DO

BE PREPARED:

If you're traveling in a dry area—especially if there are warnings of sandstorms—keep a lookout for them. Carry a safety kit, with eye goggles, a breathing mask, and a supply of drinking water.

IF YOU SEE A SANDSTORM COMING:

Run inside a building, and close all the doors and windows. If you're in a car, you might be able get away from the storm if it is a long way off. If it closes in, drive the car off the road. Close the windows and air vents, and turn off the lights (as they can make another car try to follow you). Stay put until the storm passes.

IF YOU'RE ON FOOT:

Protect your eyes with goggles or glasses, and put on a breathing mask or tie a wet bandanna or scarf around your face. Avoid low ground, and shelter behind a rock. As the storm passes, curl up on the ground and cover your head with your arms.

A haboob, a type of sandstorm featuring a fast-moving wall of sand and dust, moves in on a livestock market in Sudan.

DID YOU KNOW? Camels are used to sandstorms. They just close their eyes and nostrils. A camel can provide shelter if it sits down; you can curl up beside it.

SAND COLLAPSE

A sandy beach or dune might not look dangerous, but if sand falls on top of you, it can be very serious. If you don't get out fast, you can run out of air. Seaside and desert sand dunes can drop sand on people unexpectedly. They can also fall down if you try to dig into them to make a tunnel or cave. Even digging a big hole on the beach can be dangerous. If the hole is deep, the sides can suddenly cave in and cover you with sand.

WHAT TO DO

BE SAFE AROUND SAND:
Avoid sand dunes during storms and high winds, and watch out for safety signs and warnings in sand dune areas. Never dig under a sand dune. On the beach, don't dig big holes in the sand.

IF SAND FALLS ON YOU:
If you see it coming, try to jump out of the way. If sand is landing on you, curl into a ball and cup your hands over your face to make a breathing space. Try to stay calm and wait for help.

IF SAND FALLS ON SOMEONE ELSE:
You need to dig them out as fast as possible. Yell for help and get as many people as you can to dig with you. Meanwhile, ask someone to call an ambulance.

DANGER RATING

RISK RATING: ☠ ☠
There are sand accidents every year, but you can reduce the risk if you know how to prevent them.

SURVIVAL RATING: 30%
Being trapped under sand is very dangerous indeed—you need to get out fast to survive.

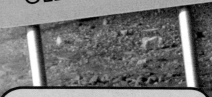

DANGER
THIS AREA IS LIABLE TO COLLAPSE FROM OLD MINEWORK

TOP TIP! It's OK to dig in sand to fill a bucket or make a sandcastle moat. But to be safe, make sure the holes are no deeper than knee high.

DUST DEVIL

A dust devil is a spinning spiral of wind that picks up dust or sand as it whirls along. It is similar to a tornado, except that dust devils usually form in hot, clear weather.

Dust devils are usually small—sometimes only as big as a person—and most are not harmful. But sometimes they can be bigger—up to 300 feet (91 m) wide and as much as 1,000 feet (305 m) high. The strong wind and fast-flying particles in a dust devil can be dangerous.

DANGER RATING

RISK RATING: ☠ ☠ ☠
Dust devils are quite common in warm, dry areas.

SURVIVAL RATING: 95%
Dust devils have been known to harm people, but it's unlikely.

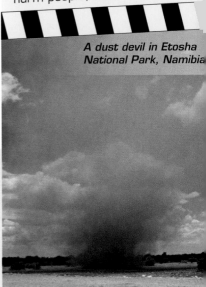

A dust devil in Etosha National Park, Namibia

WHAT TO DO

DUST DEVIL CONDITIONS:
Dust devils are most likely to form in dry, flat places during hot, still weather. They happen when the sun heats up the ground, causing a column of hot air to rise upward. So keep a lookout for them in hot, calm, dry, or desert areas.

IF YOU SEE A DUST DEVIL:
A dust devil looks like a tall spinning column or funnel of dust or sand. If you see one, you may be tempted to look more closely, but it's best to stay away—just in case. Shelter inside a building or vehicle, and watch from a safe distance.

IF YOU'RE CAUGHT IN A DUST DEVIL:
As in any sandstorm, crouch down and cover your face and head. If your car accidentally drives into a dust devil, slow down, and stop until it has passed by.

DID YOU KNOW?

Dust devils go by several different names. A dust devil can also be called a dancing devil, a dust whirl, or a willy-willy.

WATERSPOUT

Like a tornado or a dust devil, a waterspout is a towering, swirling wind spiral. The difference is that it happens over water, and sucks water up into it. Waterspouts can occur when a tornado forms over the ocean.

They usually form in cloudy weather because of the way warm, damp air moves over the water. They are found on lakes or on the sea, usually close to the shore. The main danger from waterspouts is that they can upturn boats or swamp them with water.

WHAT TO DO

IF YOU SEE A WATERSPOUT:

If you're in a boat, turn it around and sail away from the waterspout. If possible, go back to shore, as more waterspouts could form. Life rafts should be ready to launch. Stay in a cabin if possible, as a waterspout could upturn the boat or wash you overboard.

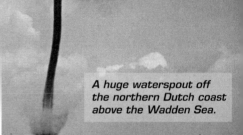

A huge waterspout off the northern Dutch coast above the Wadden Sea.

IF YOU'RE SWIMMING:

Swim away from the waterspout and get out of the water as soon as you can. If you are very close to a waterspout, try to stay calm. Tread water gently to save energy, and hold your breath if water swirls over you. Swim for the shore as soon as you can.

DANGER RATING

RISK RATING: ☠ ☠ ☠

Waterspouts are well known in tropical areas, and can happen around the world.

SURVIVAL RATING: 90%

A waterspout can easily sink a boat, but you should be able to get away from it first.

SEA MONSTERS

Long ago, sailors' reports of waterspouts may have given rise to legends about giant sea serpents attacking boats.

LIGHTNING

Lightning is one of the most spectacular events in nature. It's a giant electric spark, crackling between the clouds and the ground. It carries a huge amount of electrical energy — sometimes over 100 million volts—and can be as hot as 54,000°F, or 30,000°C—six times hotter than the surface of the Sun. And that means being struck by lightning can give someone a deadly electric shock.

DANGER RATING

RISK RATING: ☠ ☠
Thunderstorms and lightning are common, but being struck by lightning is pretty unlikely.

SURVIVAL RATING: 75%
About three quarters of people who are struck by lightning survive, though they may not always make a full recovery.

A lightning storm strikes downtown Los Angeles.

WHAT TO DO

DON'T RISK A STRIKE: Lightning happens during thunderstorms, and there will usually be a weather warning. Don't go out hiking, boating, or playing sports in a thunderstorm or if one is in the forecast.

DURING A THUNDERSTORM:
Stay indoors, and stay away from doors and windows, water, metal objects, and electrical appliances. Do not use phones or headphones—if lightning strikes the house, electricity could flow through them.

DID YOU KNOW?

Roy Sullivan, a park ranger from Virginia, U.S.A., survived being struck by lightning seven times between 1942 and 1977.

IF YOU'RE STUCK OUTDOORS:
Avoid water, high ground, and open spaces, trees, and tents. Try to find shelter in a building or a car. Don't touch any metal. If there's no shelter, crouch down with your feet together and put your hands over your ears.

BALL LIGHTNING

The phenomenon known as ball lightning is very strange and little understood. It usually appears as a glowing, floating ball, around 6–12 inches (15–30 cm) across. It may float around for up to a minute, before disappearing with a popping sound or a small explosion.

Ball lightning can happen during thunderstorms, but has been recorded in normal weather, too. It has been seen from buildings, boats, submarines, and aircraft. Scientists think it has something to do with electricity, but they don't know exactly what it is.

WHAT TO DO

IF YOU SEE BALL LIGHTNING:

Stay calm, and move away from the lightning slowly and carefully. Don't panic and run away wildly or run backward!—you could trip and get hurt.

There's not much point shutting yourself away in another room, as ball lightning can move through solid doors and walls. Instead, watch the lightning to make sure it doesn't get too close to you. It will most likely float away and disappear after a few seconds.

One of the very few existing photographs of ball lightning.

LAB LIGHTNING

Scientists are trying to create ball lightning artificially, by running electrical energy through various substances. They have succeeded in making several small glowing balls.

Temperatures reached 106°F (41.1 in New Jersey in 2006.

HEAT WAVE

A heat wave is a period of unusually hot summer weather, 10 degrees or more above average. A combination of sunshine, lack of wind, and high humidity (moisture in the air) drives the temperature up.

Heat waves are often worse in cities. In the countryside, plants and trees have a cooling effect and the temperature falls at night. But in cities, buildings and roads store heat all night long. Hot weather might not sound dangerous, but heat waves can actually cause thousands of deaths.

DANGER RATING

RISK RATING: 💀 💀 💀
Heat waves are a danger every summer, and some experts think they are getting worse.

SURVIVAL RATING: 90%
Of the people affected by a heat wave, most will survive. But if heat waves affect whole countries, they can claim many lives.

WHAT TO DO

IF A HEAT WAVE IS PREDICTED:
Don't plan any strenuous activities, such as hiking, sports, or building projects. Stock up on sunscreen and make sure you have a sunhat. Keep emergency numbers handy.

DURING A HEAT WAVE:
Stay indoors in the middle of the day. Use air-conditioning if you have it, or if not, close curtains, open windows, and use fans to keep your house cool. Drink lots of water and cold drinks—but avoid coffee, strong tea, and alcohol, as they can make your body lose water. Outdoors, wear a hat and long, light, loose clothing. Slow down, and avoid running around.

IF SOMEONE GETS TOO HOT
People can die during heat waves from overheating—especially the old, young, or unwell. The signs include feeling hot, sick, and dizzy, a red rash and no sweating. If this happens, call an ambulance. Use cold water to cool them down.

DROUGHT

A drought is an unusually dry period, often caused by low rainfall. Droughts can have other causes, too, such as people using up too much water for watering crops.

In most countries, droughts last for a few weeks or months, but the rain eventually returns. Very severe droughts, however, can cause disaster, especially in developing countries, where people may be very poor and have nowhere else to move to. A long-term drought can destroy crops and lead to a deadly famine (food shortage) as well as dangerous water shortages.

DANGER RATING

RISK RATING: ☠ ☠ ☠
Droughts are a normal part of weather patterns.

SURVIVAL RATING: 90%
It's unlikely you'll experience a really dangerous drought.

In drought areas, like here in Mali, water supplies are used over and over, allowing diseases to spread.

WHAT TO DO

IF A DROUGHT IS PREDICTED:
Try to reduce the amount of water you use. Don't leave taps running, have quick showers or shallow baths, and avoid watering your lawn or garden.

DURING A DROUGHT:
You still need to save water, but make sure you drink enough. The weather will be dry and probably very hot, making you sweat, so you need to drink a lot. If water is really short, save it all for drinking—don't waste it on washing. Listen for official instructions in case you are told to leave the area. Droughts can also lead to other problems such as wildfires and dust storms, so be on your guard.

TOP TIP! One good way to save water is to catch rainwater in a bucket. It can then be used for watering plants.

LOST IN THE DESERT

Deserts are very dry areas where few things can survive. Some are almost all bare rock or sand; others may have small bushes or cacti growing in them. Most deserts are hot during the day, but get cold at night. In some countries, such as the U.S.A. and Australia, a lot of roads run through deserts—drivers can lose their way and cars can break down.

WHAT TO DO

DESERT SAFETY:

If you're going to travel in a desert area, make sure you take some spare fuel, high-energy foods, blankets, a map, sun hats and sunglasses, and lots of water.

IF YOU GET LOST:

If you're in a car that breaks down, stay with the car. It will be too hot inside, so sit beside it in the shade. Sit on a box or stool, not on the ground, as the ground will be much hotter than the air. Keep covered up with long, loose clothing and a hat. At night, snuggle up inside the car, wrapped in blankets. Drink as much water as you need. If you're lost on foot, look for

DANGER RATING

RISK RATING: ☠ ☠

Most journeys are uneventful, but deserts are dangerous.

SURVIVAL RATING: 60%

Humans can only survive 3 or 4 days without water—if you run out, you're in serious danger. If people know you're missing, you should be found in time.

trees, rocks, or cliffs that could provide shade.

SIGNAL FOR HELP:

If you have a cell phone, use it to call for help. Arrange branches or stones in a large triangle shape (an international SOS signal), or simply spell SOS. Use a small mirror or any shiny object to reflect the sun to signal to passing aircraft.

LOST AT THE POLES

Explorers battle through the ice and snow on their way to the South Pole.

The poles are the extreme northerly and southerly points of Earth, farthest away from the equator. The regions around the poles are freezing cold, and often covered with ice and snow and scoured by howling winds. Few people go there at all, but you could get lost there if a vehicle breaks down during an expedition, or if you're in a plane that crashes.

WHAT TO DO

IF YOU CRASH OR BREAK DOWN:

Try to phone or radio for help. Create an SOS signal using whatever you can—bags, boxes, or vehicle parts. Everyone should stay together and stay with the vehicle, using it as shelter. Don't wander off— you could fall down a crevasse or into icy water, or get buried in snow. Keep your body covered up, and huddle together with other people. If you have any fuel, make a fire and melt snow to make drinking water. Avoid melting ice or snow in your mouth—it will make you even colder.

DANGER RATING

RISK RATING: ☠
Few people go to the poles except on well-organized, official trips, so getting lost is rare.

SURVIVAL RATING: 20%
It's so cold at the poles that surviving when lost is tough.

HOW COLD? The average temperature in the Arctic (the area around the North Pole) is about -8°F (-22°C). In the Antarctic, around the South Pole, it's even colder at around -58°F (-50°C).

LOST ON A MOUNTAIN

Lots of people go hiking, climbing, rafting, and skiing in mountain areas, and have lots of fun. But mountains can be scary and dangerous, too. They have steep slopes and cliffs, strong winds, and sometimes snow and ice. People often get lost, separated from their group, or stuck because of an injury such as a twisted ankle.

DANGER RATING

RISK RATING: ☠ ☠ ☠
A lot of people visit mountains, and people get lost or injured quite often.

SURVIVAL RATING: 70%
It depends on the mountain. On some, getting lost is disastrous—but on most, you'll probably be rescued.

WHAT TO DO

MOUNTAIN SAFETY:
Be prepared before you go up into the mountains. Wear hiking boots and outdoor clothes, and take drinks, snacks, a whistle, and a warm, windproof coat. Plan your route, and tell someone where you will be and when you'll be back. Check the forecast—don't set out if it's bad.

IF YOU'RE LOST:
Your map might help you, or the view may show you a safe route down the mountain. If it's daylight and good weather, you can probably walk to safety. Follow valleys and streams downhill.

Retreating down an icy cliff in a blizzard is extremely difficult and dangerous.

IF YOU GET STUCK:
Bad weather, nightfall, or an injury can trap you on a mountain. Look for a place to shelter, such as between rocks, and call for help on a cell phone if possible. If not, blow your whistle (or make a whistling noise) three times, wait a minute then blow it again. Huddle up and wait for rescue.

TOP TIP! If you see a rescue helicopter, you can signal to it that you need help by sticking your arms up and out in a big 'Y' shape.

FALLEN INTO A VOLCANIC CRATER

A volcano's crater is the bowl-shaped hollow at the top, where lava and rocks burst out during an eruption. Craters are usually round with steep sides and a flat bottom. Some active volcanoes are considered safe for tourists to visit, so there are trails leading up to the edge of the crater—and sometimes, people fall in.

WHAT TO DO

NO CRATER CRAZINESS!

Volcanoes are so exciting that tourists sometimes climb over safety barriers, or clamber down inside the edge of a crater, to get a better look and take photos. Never, ever do this! The steep slopes and loose rocks mean you can slip easily.

DID YOU KNOW?

Volcanoes can be "dormant"—which means "sleeping"—for many years, then suddenly become active and start erupting again.

IF YOU FALL IN:

Drop anything you're holding and use your arms and legs to try to steady yourself. When you come to a stop, keep still and wave and call to people on the edge of the crater to get help. Don't get up and try to climb back out by yourself—you could fall again. And some craters contain dangerous hot lava, hot water, or steam jets that could seriously injure you. Stay calm and wait to be rescued.

The crater of an active volcano in Ethiopia.

DANGER RATING

RISK RATING: ☠ ☠

Volcano craters are not safe places to be, but most people avoid danger by acting sensibly.

SURVIVAL RATING: 50%

If you do fall into a crater, you'll probably need a lot of luck and help to get out safely.

SWEPT AWAY IN A RIVER

Rivers are often far more dangerous than they look. There may be strong currents and overhanging ledges under the surface. Water that doesn't seem to be flowing very fast can still carry you away quickly. And if there are rocks in the river, you could be thrown against them. It's important to take care near dangerous rivers and avoid being swept away in the first place.

DANGER RATING

RISK RATING: ☠ ☠ ☠
Even rivers that look calm and safe can sweep people away.

SURVIVAL RATING: 40%
Being swept away by a river is extremely dangerous.

Fast-flowing rivers like this, the Brathay in England's Lake District, are especially dangerous.

WHAT TO DO

RIVER SAFETY:

Near rivers, stay away from the bank—don't lean over to try to peer in, touch the water, or grab something you've dropped. Watch out for wet, slippery rocks and muddy banks. Don't try to wade across a river instead of using a bridge. And don't swim or paddle in rivers, except at well-known safe swimming places, with sensible adults or with an organized group.

IF YOU ARE SWEPT AWAY:

Don't try to struggle against the current—you'll wear yourself out. Instead, stay calm, and swim sideways, aiming for the nearest bank, as you are swept along. Try to steer around rocks. If you can, climb out of the river and move away from the edge. Otherwise, grab on to a branch or rock on the bank. Shout for help, hang on tight, and wait to be rescued.

WATER POWER Rushing water just 12 inches (30 cm) deep is enough to sweep you off your feet and carry you away.

SWEPT OVER A WATERFALL

People are swept over waterfalls every year—few survive. Waterfalls occur where a river plunges over a ledge of hard rock. Often the falling water has worn away a deep pool at the base. Even if the fall is not high, it can be hard to escape from the churning pool.

WHAT TO DO

DON'T LET IT HAPPEN:
Never swim, play, or paddle in water upstream from a waterfall. Avoid standing on the bank or rocks near the top of a waterfall, close to the water's edge.

IF YOU ARE SWEPT AWAY:
Try to get out of the water at once, or grab a rock, branch, or tree root and hold on until you are rescued. If you are swept over the waterfall, cover your head and hold your breath. After you land, kick upward to try to reach the surface, and let the river carry you away from the waterfall. Swim for the bank once you are in calmer water.

DANGER RATING

RISK RATING: ☠ ☠
Even if you do fall into a river, you probably won't be near a waterfall.

SURVIVAL RATING: 20%
People have survived going over waterfalls, but they are the minority.

The Money Drop Waterfall in Rock Creek, Washington.

DID YOU KNOW?

In 1960, a 7-year-old boy named Roger Woodward miraculously survived being swept over one of the world's most powerful waterfalls, Niagara Falls. He was wearing a life vest and was rescued from the plunge pool by a tour boat.

LOST AT SEA IN A BOAT OR RAFT

You could end up adrift at sea for several reasons. You could be in a small motorboat that breaks down, or you could run out of fuel and lose your way. Or you could be on a bigger boat or ship that sinks, leaving you in a lifeboat or life raft. The dangers you face include cold and wind, sunburn, and water shortages.

WHAT TO DO

KEEP WARM:
Wrap up in all the clothes you have, including wet suits and diving suits. Shelter from the wind.

AVOID THE SUN:
If there is strong sunshine, you could get bad sunburn or sunstroke. Shade yourself with a hat, sheet, or tarpaulin.

COLLECT WATER:
Water is more important than food—only eat if you have water to drink, too, as digesting food uses up water in your body. Drink the fresh water you have when you need to. Use any containers you have to collect rainwater, and store it carefully. If you find chunks of ice in the sea, you can melt them and drink them, as they should not be salty. Do not drink seawater, unless your raft has equipment for making it safe.

DANGER RATING

RISK RATING: ☠ ☠ ☠
People get lost at sea quite often, though they are usually rescued.

SURVIVAL RATING: 75%
In most cases, someone will be looking for you, and you have a good chance of survival.

GET HELP:
If you see a ship or aircraft, send a signal with distress flares, a mirror to reflect the sunlight, or a flashlight at night. If you see land, paddle toward it with your hands or bits of wood.

TOP TIP! Before collecting rain in a tarpaulin or plastic sheet, rinse it in the sea. Otherwise, the buildup of salt on it from the sea spray will make your water salty.

ADRIFT AT SEA WITH NO BOAT

What if your boat sinks and you're left on your own in the open ocean? This situation is, of course, incredibly hazardous. But there's a lot you can do to make it safer. The most important thing to do is stay calm and save as much energy as you can.

DANGER RATING

RISK RATING: ☠ ☠

It's very unlikely this will happen, as most boats have life rafts.

SURVIVAL RATING: 30%

People do survive this situation, though they may have to wait in the sea for a long time.

WHAT TO DO

IF YOUR BOAT IS SINKING:

Try to grab something that will help you stay afloat, such as a life jacket or pieces of wooden wreckage. Once you are in the water, move away from the boat, as it can suck you downward when it sinks.

IS IT A SHARK?

Don't worry if you feel something touching you in the water—it's probably NOT a shark. Shark attacks are actually quite rare. It's probably a smaller fish or even a friendly dolphin. Dolphins have been known to surround and support people stranded in the water.

STAY AFLOAT:

If you don't have a float, you may be able to make one by inflating a pair of trousers or a top. Tie up the arm or leg openings and blow air into the waist, then hold it closed. You may need to keep refilling it. Meanwhile, tread water slowly and calmly— don't panic. Save your energy for keeping you warm, and for shouting and waving if you see a boat.

Keep looking out for other floating objects that you can use.

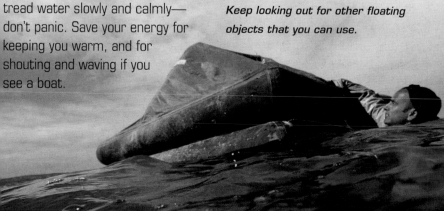

CAUGHT IN A WHIRLPOOL

Moskstraumen in Norway is one of the world's most powerful whirlpools.

A whirlpool is a spiraling body of water in a sea, lake, or river. It can also be called a maelstrom or vortex, especially if the water is sucked downward as well as going round and round.

Whirlpools usually form where fast-moving tides, or one river flowing into another, cause the water to flow in a huge spiral.

WHAT TO DO

IF YOU SEE A WHIRLPOOL:

If you see water moving in a swirling, churning pattern, stay away! Don't swim in the water, even in a different part of the river or bay. Boats should not go near the whirlpool—even large boats.

IF YOUR BOAT IS SUCKED IN:

The boat may lean to one side and spin around before starting to capsize. People have survived whirlpools by jumping off the boat and swimming to shore. It's usually safer to stay with the boat—stay up on deck in case it sinks.

IF YOU'RE IN A WHIRLPOOL WITH NO BOAT:

Tread water and look out for floating objects to hold on to. Paddle away from the middle of the whirlpool and call for help.

MYTHICAL MAELSTROM

In the Greek myth *The Odyssey*, the hero Odysseus must sail between Charybdis, a sea monster who creates whirlpools, and Scylla, a many-headed monster, to make his way home.

DANGER RATING

RISK RATING: ☠

Dangerous whirlpools are extremely rare.

SURVIVAL RATING: 60%

If you do end up in a whirlpool, things could get nasty, but you do have a reasonable chance of escape.

WASHED ASHORE ON A REMOTE ISLAND

If you fall off a boat or get shipwrecked, seeing an island where you can swim ashore is good news!

WHAT TO DO

MAKE IT ASHORE:

Aim for a gently sloping, sandy beach in a small bay, if possible. Swim toward the flattest part of the beach—this will make it easier to walk ashore. Try to stay in the trough between two waves. If a wave is about to break over you, turn to face it, dive under it, and come up in the trough behind it, then aim for the shore again. Once ashore, move far up the beach and make sure the tide can't cut you off.

FIND WATER AND FOOD:

You may find fresh water in a stream flowing into the sea, in pools among sand dunes, or trickling over rocks or cliffs behind the beach. Don't drink seawater—it will make you ill.

DANGER RATING

RISK RATING: ☠ ☠
This situation may happen a lot in films or cartoons, but it's very unusual in real life!

SURVIVAL RATING: 70%
If you're lucky enough to make it to dry land, you should survive.

Rock pools may contain fish, crabs, limpets, and abalone. Tropical islands may also have coconut and avocado trees.

FIND SHELTER:

Look for a cave (check it doesn't get cut off by the tide), or make a shelter by leaning branches and large leaves against a rock or tree.

EXPLORE THE ISLAND:

Walk around the island to look for food sources and campsites. Even uninhabited islands may have shelters left by previous visitors.

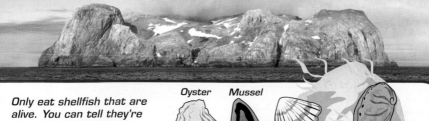

Only eat shellfish that are alive. You can tell they're alive if their shells are very hard to open.

Oyster   Mussel

Limpet   Abalone

LOST IN A CAVE

In many parts of the world, there are vast networks of cave passageways and chambers deep underground. Scientists studying wildlife and rocks, and cavers or spelunkers (people who go into caves for sport) explore them, and tourists can also go on cave tours. It's possible that you could get lost on a tour, or cut off by water or a rockfall.

WHAT TO DO

STAY TOGETHER, STAY WARM, AND STAY STILL:

Caves are full of dangers—cliffs, sharp rocks, and underground rivers and pools. And they are usually very, very dark. If you don't know your way, it's safer to stay still and wait to be found. If you are in a group, everyone should huddle together for warmth. Put on all the spare clothes, gloves, and hats you have to keep as warm as you can. Stay away from cave water, as getting wet will make you colder.

MAKE CONTACT:

If you have a cell phone, use it to call for help. If it doesn't work, try again later. If you hear rescuers coming, call to them and shine flashlights to help them find you.

SAVE BATTERIES:

Stuck in the pitch blackness of a deep cave, you'll probably want to switch on your flashlight. But it's better to keep it switched off and save the batteries for emergencies or for signaling to rescuers. The same goes for your cell phone—switch it off when it's not in use, to save the batteries.

TOP TIP! If your flashlight runs out of batteries or you don't have one, a cell phone can be used to shine a small amount of light.

STUCK ON A CLIFF FACE

Cliffs are very dangerous places. People can get hurt by falling off them, or by trying to climb up them without proper safety equipment. Even experienced climbers with ropes sometimes get stuck and have to be rescued. Rescuers sometimes climb the cliff using ropes to help the trapped person down, or they can use a rescue helicopter to airlift them to safety.

WHAT TO DO

CLIFF SENSE:
Be very, very careful near cliffs. Don't go near cliff edges, and never try to climb a cliff without proper ropes and an expert guide—unless you're escaping from another emergency, such as a shipwreck!

IF YOU GET STUCK:
You could get stuck on a cliff by falling down from the top, or by climbing up from the bottom. Wherever you are, try to lean in toward the cliff face, staying back from the edge of the rock or ledge you are on. Keep still, and breathe steadily. If you need to wave or shout for help, do so calmly and slowly.

STEEP SLOPES

You might think of a cliff as a vertical drop, but many cliffs are more like very steep slopes. If you fall down, you may be able to slide to a halt or stop on a ledge.

A rescuer dangles from a helicopter to save a boy from a cliff ledge.

DANGER RATING

RISK RATING: ☠ ☠ ☠
All cliffs are dangerous, especially when people aren't careful enough.

SURVIVAL RATING: 80%
If you're stuck on a cliff face, rescue will probably be coming soon.

IF YOU ARE INJURED:
Try to stop any bleeding by pressing your hand onto the wound. Keep any suspected broken bones as still as you can.

OUT ON THIN ICE

If possible, you should avoid walking over ice at all if you don't have to. But even if you try to avoid it, you could still end up on the ice after a fall or traffic accident. Ice more than 4 inches (10 cm) thick can support a person's weight. But even if the ice you are on feels safe, there could be thinner areas, especially on frozen rivers, and you could fall through.

DANGER RATING

RISK RATING: ☠ ☠ ☠ ☠ ☠
In many places, water freezes over every winter and it's easy to get into trouble.

SURVIVAL RATING: 90%
If you get off the ice quickly, you should be safe.

WHAT TO DO

DON'T RISK IT:

Don't be tempted to step out onto a frozen lake or river to see what happens. And don't decide to go onto the ice for just a second to retrieve a ball or bag—it can still break. People do activities such as ice fishing on very thick ice, but this is only safe when the ice has been carefully tested.

IF YOU ARE ON THIN ICE:

Lie down and spread out your arms and legs to spread your weight. Slither or roll toward the edge of the ice. Avoid ice that is cracked and aim for thicker ice—it looks clearer and bluer than thin ice. If you are on a section of ice surrounded by breaking ice, don't move. Lie still and shout for help.

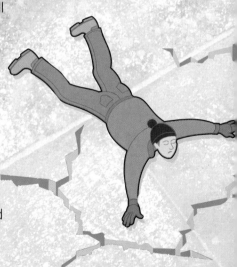

DOG DISASTERS People sometimes risk their lives going onto thin ice to catch their runaway dog. Never do this! Remember you are probably heavier than your dog. On top of that, dogs can often scramble to safety themselves, even if they have fallen through the ice.

FALLEN THROUGH ICE

Falling through ice is very dangerous as the water underneath is icy cold. People can only survive in freezing cold water for a few minutes before they get too cold and numb to move. It's also possible to fall through a hole in the ice, then get trapped under the solid ice nearby and drown. It's vital to get out as soon as you can.

WHAT TO DO

AS YOU FALL:

If you feel yourself falling, lean back to help keep your head above water. The cold water will shock you and make you gasp, but stay as calm as you can and tread water.

TRY TO GET OUT:

Turn to face the direction you came from, as this is probably the strongest ice. Put your arms on the ice, lean forward and kick your legs behind you to try to "swim" out of the hole. You may need to rest halfway, with your upper body on the ice and your legs still in the water. Push against the other side of the hole. If the ice breaks, move forward and try again.

IF SOMEONE ELSE FALLS IN:

People often die going onto the ice to save someone else who has fallen through. Instead, rescuers should throw a rope, or scarves tied together, and pull the person out. If there's no rope, a long pole or plank may help the person to pull him or herself out. If going onto the ice is essential, the rescuer should tie a rope around his or her waist, with the other end tied to something on shore, and crawl, not walk, across the ice.

TOP TIP! You may be able to stick keys, jewelry, or a penknife into the ice to help pull yourself out.

DANGER RATING

RISK RATING: ☠ ☠ ☠
You should be able to avoid falling through ice, but sadly it happens to hundreds of people each year.

SURVIVAL RATING: 30%
It's difficult to survive unless you can get out of the water fast.

SINKING IN QUICKSAND

This young elephant waded into the waterhole to get a drink, but got stuck in the quicksand.

DANGER RATING

RISK RATING: ☠ ☠
Dangerous quicksand is rare.

SURVIVAL RATING: 90%
It's fairly easy to escape from quicksand, as long as you know what to do.

In adventure films, quicksand can suck people under in seconds. In real life, it's not really all that bad. Quicksand can form anywhere where sand, or sandy, silty mud, gets saturated with water. This can create a loose, semiliquid substance that you can sink into. However, you can float in quicksand, just as you can in water, so you're unlikely to go under.

WHAT TO DO

AVOID QUICKSAND:
Look out for quicksand when walking on beaches and other sandy areas. It's hard to see from a distance, but when you step on it, it may wobble and ripple like jelly—if it does, step back. You can also use a long pole to test for quicksand.

IF YOU GET STUCK IN QUICKSAND:
If you walk over quicksand, you may start to sink downward. Drop any heavy bags you are carrying and if possible, try to kick off your shoes. Lean over and lie down on your back—try to do this before you sink any deeper than waist height! While "floating" on your back, you can slowly drag your legs and feet back up to the surface. Once you're out, roll or wriggle away over the surface of the quicksand to safety.

TOP TIP! The more quicksand vibrates and shakes about, the more liquid it gets. When you are sinking, panicking and thrashing around may make you sink faster. But when you are pulling your legs out, it may help to shake and wiggle them.

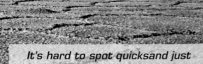

It's hard to spot quicksand just by looking at it—it often looks like normal sand.

STUCK IN A SWAMP

A swamp is a wet, soggy area with a combination of mud, water, and marshy ground. There are usually trees, grasses, and water plants. It can be very hard to find your way through a swamp, as you can't see far and you can easily wander into waist-deep water. Worst of all, you can sink into sticky mud and get trapped.

WHAT TO DO

SWAMP SAFETY:

It's a good idea to avoid swamps, unless you're with an organized group or a knowledgeable guide. But if you are in one, the best way to stay safe is to step on tufts of grass and bunches of water reeds. If you can find a long stick, use it to test the ground before you step on it. Avoid pools and flat, muddy areas where you could sink.

IF YOU GET STUCK:

If you feel yourself sinking into mud, lie down quickly so that you float, and swim or roll to firmer ground. If you react too slowly and your feet get stuck, you might be able to pull yourself out by grabbing a tree branch.

IF YOU'RE LOST:

If other people know where you are and will come looking for you, find a safe place to wait. If you can do so safely, climb a tree. It will keep you away from swamp animals such as crocodiles, and it will make it easier to wave to rescue helicopters.

DANGER RATING

RISK RATING: ☠ ☠
Swamps are hard to travel in, so it's unlikely you'll get lost in one.

SURVIVAL RATING: 60%
Escaping from a swamp could be difficult, especially if it's full of crocodiles.

SWAMP SURVIVOR

In 2007, an Australian farmer was stranded in a crocodile-infested swamp after his horse carried him the wrong way. He was found by a search helicopter after spending seven nights in a tree!

CUT OFF BY THE TIDE

Tides exist at the coast because of the gravity of the moon. It pulls at the sea, making it rise up the beach and then fall back down twice a day. Sometimes, you can reach a sheltered bay, island, or sea cave at low tide by walking along the beach, but when high tide comes, the route is cut off by the rising water. You may become trapped between the rising tide and high cliffs.

WHAT TO DO

WATCH THE TIDES:

At the beach, always keep an eye on where you are and how close the tide is. Move away from areas that could be cut off while the tide is still out. You can often check in advance when the tide will come in, at bulletin boards on the beach. Tide timetables are sometimes posted on the Internet, too.

IF YOU ARE CUT OFF:

Call for help as soon as you can. If you have a phone, call the emergency services and ask for the coast guard, who may rescue you by boat or helicopter. You can also try to get help by shouting to anyone you can see on the land or in a boat.

DANGER RATING

RISK RATING: ☠ ☠ ☠ ☠
People get cut off by the tide all the time. It can happen very quickly with little warning.

SURVIVAL RATING: 90%
If you raise the alarm fast, you'll probably be rescued.

Twenty-one Chinese migrant workers died in Morecambe Bay, England, in 2005 when they were caught by fast rising tides as they searched for cockles, a shellfish delicacy.

TOP TIP! Avoid playing or exploring in caves on the beach. The tide could come in while you are inside and can't see it coming.

CAUGHT IN A RIPTIDE

A riptide is not a tide, but a strong current of water flowing from the beach out into the sea. It can also be called a rip current, or a rip. A riptide forms when water brought ashore by breaking waves gathers and flows back into the sea along a narrow channel. Riptides can sweep swimmers out to sea, but only a short distance.

Surfers use riptides to get a lift out to deeper water.

DANGER RATING

RISK RATING: ☠ ☠ ☠ ☠
Riptides are very common and thousands and thousands of people are caught in them every year.

SURVIVAL RATING: 90%
You should be able to survive a riptide if you know what to do.

WHAT TO DO

AVOID RIPTIDES:

You can sometimes spot a riptide. The water in the current may look calmer, flatter, and darker than the surrounding waves. You should also avoid swimming at low tide, when riptides are more common. And don't swim close to piers and jetties, as riptides often form there.

IF YOU'RE CAUGHT IN THE CURRENT:

When you feel the water sweeping you away, don't panic. People usually only drown in riptides if they struggle and try to swim against the current. Instead, tread water calmly until the current stops, then swim back to the shore. Or, if you're a good swimmer, you can try swimming sideways, along the beach, to escape from the current.

RIPPING ALONG

The water in a riptide can flow at a speed of up to 6 mph (10 kph). This is quite a slow speed if you're running, but it's much faster than you can swim.

LOST ON A GLACIER

A glacier is a massive, slow-moving river of ice. Glaciers form in cold places, such as high mountains, where heavy snowfall packs down into solid ice over time. Mountaineers often have to cross glaciers when they climb high mountains, and skiers often ski over snow-covered glaciers, too. As well as being cold, glaciers are dangerous because of the deep cracks, or crevasses, that form in them.

DANGER RATING

RISK RATING: ☠ ☠
Glacier climbing is usually done in organized groups, so you shouldn't get lost.

SURVIVAL RATING: 60%
If you do get well and truly lost on a glacier, you'll need skill and luck to reach safety.

WHAT TO DO

GLACIER SAFETY:
You should only venture onto a glacier in a properly led group with an experienced guide, carrying climbing ropes and equipment. Always follow the leader's instructions and stay roped together with everyone else.

IF YOU GET LOST:
You still could end up on a glacier after getting lost on a mountain, or after a plane crash. If the glacier is snowy, snow could cover the crevasses and make them invisible, so it's best to stay still. Call for help, and wrap up warm in all the clothing you have with you. If there's no snow and you can see the crevasses clearly, you can move away from them and aim sideways to get off the glacier. If you are skiing and get lost on a glacier, keep your skis on, as they spread your weight over a bigger area and make you less likely to fall down a crevasse.

TOP TIP! You should always wear crampons when walking on a glacier. These are special spikes that fit on to your boots to help your feet grip the ice.

FALLEN DOWN A CREVASSE

Crevasses are scary and very dangerous. Some are just a few feet deep, but others are much deeper—as deep as the glacier itself, which can be over 330 feet (100 m) thick. Falling down a crevasse can be deadly. If you survive the fall, you could be injured and will probably have to depend on other climbers to get you out.

WHAT TO DO

BE PREPARED:
Sensible climbers always cross crevasses in groups, roped together so that if one person falls down a crevasse, the others can pull him or her out. You should always wear a climbing helmet, as many people who fall down crevasses get head injuries.

IF YOU FALL:
If you're on a rope, you may be able to climb out or be pulled out by the other climbers. If you're not, you'll fall to the bottom of the crevasse. Try to stay in a safe place, away from any deeper cracks you can see. Wrap up well and curl up in a ball to keep warm while you wait for rescue. Call to people on the surface to let them know where you are.

If you're alone, your only hope is to move along the bottom of the crevasse to see if you can find a way out. Some crevasses slope back up to the surface, or lead out of a hole in the side of the glacier.

DANGER RATING

RISK RATING: ☠☠
Though falling down a crevasse isn't very common, crevasses do claim lives every year.

SURVIVAL RATING: 50%
Falling down a cevasse is serious, but having climbing ropes will improve your chances.

MIRACLE ESCAPE In 1985, a climber named Joe Simpson fell down a crevasse in Peru. Though he had a broken leg, he managed to crawl out of the crevasse and down the glacier to safety.

LOST IN THE JUNGLE

The word "jungle" is usually used to mean a rain forest—a type of thick, humid, rainy forest found in the tropical regions of the world. Rain forests can be dangerous as they are home to lots of biting bugs and large wild animals.

WHAT TO DO

TRAVEL SAFELY:

You should not try to walk through a tropical jungle except along a clear tourist trail, or with an experienced guide. However, if you do go into the jungle, be prepared. Wear strong boots and take clothing with full-length arms and legs, snacks, a water bottle, a raincoat, a penknife, and matches.

IF YOU GET LOST:

First, shout and wave to help your travel companions find you again. If that doesn't work, you'll have to wait to be rescued. Stay in one place and wear lots of clothes to protect against biting insects. If it rains, put your coat on and try to avoid getting soaked. If you have anything brightly colored or shiny, hang it on a branch to help rescuers spot you.

DANGER RATING

RISK RATING: 💀 💀

You're unlikely to be wandering through a rain forest without a guide.

SURVIVAL RATING: 60%

It is very hard to find people in the jungle, so getting lost is NOT a good idea!

FOOD AND WATER:

Drink your own water supply first. If you need more, take water from a fast-flowing stream or spring, or collect rain in your raincoat. If you go near a stream or river, take care and watch out for crocodiles or alligators and dangerous fish. You may find fruit such as bananas, mangoes, and avocados, but only eat them if you are 100 percent sure you know what they are.

DID YOU KNOW?

In 2007, two French hikers were lost in the rain forest in French Guiana, South America, for almost two months! They survived by eating turtles and spiders.

TRAPPED BY A FALLEN TREE

A big, tall tree toppling over can be a deadly danger. A tree trunk, or even a large branch, can be so heavy that if it pins you to the ground, you'll never be able to escape on your own.

In forests, parks, and even backyards, trees can fall down when they grow old and die, or they can be blown down by heavy winds. Sometimes people get trapped when a tree they are cutting down falls on them.

DANGER RATING

RISK RATING: ☠ ☠ ☠
Falling trees kill hundreds of people every year.

SURVIVAL RATING: 75%
Being trapped by a fallen tree is dangerous and scary, but you should be rescued.

TOP TIP! No one should ever try to cut down a tree if they don't know exactly what they are doing. If a tree needs to come down, call a trained tree feller.

WHAT TO DO

IF A TREE IS FALLING:
You may be warned that a tree is about to fall by a loud creaking sound. You'll have a few seconds before it hits the ground. Stay calm, look for the tree, and figure out which way it is falling. Run out of reach or get on the other side of the tree, whichever is quickest.

IF THE TREE LANDS ON YOU:
Try to move your head and body out of the way of the tree and cover your head with your arms. If part of your body gets pinned under the tree, you may want to try to pull free, but if you're stuck fast, stop trying, as this will wear you out. Instead, stay calm and shout to passersby, or use a phone to call for help. While you wait, stay calm, and keep warm by putting on any extra clothes you have with you.

BOA CONSTRICTOR

Boas and pythons are constrictor snakes. This means that instead of giving their prey a poisonous bite, they wrap their bodies around their victims and squeeze them. As they squeeze more and more tightly, the victim cannot breathe and gets suffocated or strangled. The snake then opens its mouth wide and swallows its prey whole. Even a snake that is too small to eat a human could try to constrict and strangle someone. Constrictors are found around the world, mainly in tropical areas.

WHAT TO DO

TAKE CARE WITH SNAKES:
If you see a snake in the wild, you should avoid it. However, many people keep boas and pythons as pets, and you need to be careful with them, too. Never let a pet constrictor snake, especially a large one, coil around your body or neck.

IF A CONSTRICTOR ATTACKS:
If a constrictor wraps itself around you, stay calm, take a deep breath and hold it in. The snake will take its chance to squeeze when you breathe out. Try to control the snake's head and unwrap its body from around you.

DANGER RATING

RISK RATING: ☠ ☠
Being squeezed and swallowed by a snake is very rare, but it does happen.

SURVIVAL RATING: 60%
Most snakes are not big enough to swallow you. With help, you may be able to get away.

Get someone to help you if possible. As soon as you are free, run away from the snake or lock it in its tank or in another room.

DID YOU KNOW?

Large constrictor snakes, such as the African rock python and the reticulated python, can grow up to 26 to 33 feet (8–10 m) long.

They have been known to kill and swallow whole bears and antelopes, as well as humans.

RATTLESNAKE BITE

There are about 50 different types of rattlesnakes. They live in North, Central, and South America, especially in hot, dry areas. These very poisonous snakes get their name because they have a "rattle" on their tails, made of rings of hard, dried, dead skin. The snake can shake its rattle as a warning when it feels threatened. That's good news, because it helps you avoid rattlesnakes and stay safe. If you are bitten, you must get help fast.

WHAT TO DO

SNAKE SENSE:

If you're going to be in rattlesnake country, wear tough boots and long pants. Watch out for snakes, and don't stick your hands into bushes or holes without checking for snakes first.

KEEP YOUR DISTANCE:

If you see or hear a rattlesnake, move away from it slowly. Sudden movements could scare the snake. Never try to tease a rattlesnake, chase it, or pick it up—most bites happen because people do this!

WHAT NOT TO DO

Do not cut into the bite, try to suck the poison out, or tie a tight tourniquet or bandage around the bitten body part. These things can actually make matters a lot worse.

DANGER RATING

RISK RATING: ☠ ☠ ☠
Rattlesnakes are common in many parts of the U.S.A. and other countries.

SURVIVAL RATING: 80%
Not all rattlesnake bites are deadly, and most can be treated, so you're likely to survive.

IF YOU ARE BITTEN:

Call for help to get to a hospital as soon as you can, where you can be treated with antivenom. Sit still and stay calm, and hold the bitten part lower than your heart. Moving around increases your bloodflow and makes the poison spread. Remove all watches and jewelry in case of swelling. If possible, wash the bite with soap and water.

An Eastern diamondback, one of the most dangerous species of rattlesnake.

COBRA ATTACK

Cobras are highly poisonous snakes. There are several types of cobras, all found in southern Asia and Africa. When a cobra feels threatened, it will lift up the front of its body, and spread out the ribs behind its head, forming a distinctive, wide "hood" shape. Then, the cobra may strike its prey. Cobra venom is dangerous. It kills by paralyzing the body, making it impossible to breathe. Bites can be treated with antivenom or a medical breathing machine.

DANGER RATING

RISK RATING: ☠ ☠
Cobras do not want to bite you and will only do so if cornered. Stay calm and move away.

SURVIVAL RATING: 70%
It's possible to survive most cobra bites, except in the case of the king cobra.

WHAT TO DO

IF A COBRA REARS UP:
This means it is angry or scared and may bite. Back away immediately, and keep a distance of at least the length of the snake between it and yourself. A cobra can dart its body forward and strike suddenly.

IF YOU ARE BITTEN:
Get to a hospital as fast as possible. Stay calm, lying still and keeping the bitten body part down. Try to remember what the cobra looked like so that doctors can identify the species.

DID YOU KNOW?

Spitting cobras, which are found in Africa, can squirt venom into their victims' eyes from a distance of over 7 feet (2 m) away.

This Indian cobra is feeling threatened—stay well away!

VAMPIRE BAT

Vampire bats that suck your blood are not just found in comics and films—they really exist! There are three types of vampire bats, but only one of them attacks humans—the common vampire bat, found in Central and South America. Vampire bats feed on blood, usually from livestock, and nothing else, and they need to feed every night.

DANGER RATING

RISK RATING: ☠ ☠
Vampire bats are a risk in some South American countries.

SURVIVAL RATING: 90%
The vampire bat bite in itself is not very dangerous, but it can give you rabies. However, quick treatment can keep you safe.

The vampire bat uses its sharp front teeth to make a small, painless cut in the skin.

WHAT TO DO

PROTECT YOURSELF:
If you're in an area that has vampire bats, make sure your house, hut, or tent has no openings, and close your windows at night. Sleeping under a mosquito net will also keep bats away.

SPOT THE SIGNS:
A vampire bat's saliva contains a painkiller, so when it bites you, you don't feel it and don't wake up. It can be difficult to tell if you've been bitten. Check for any small, curved cuts or grazes on your skin.

WING WALKERS
Like other bats, vampire bats can fly, but when they get close to their victims, they land and walk, so that they can sneak up quietly. They walk by folding up their wings and using them like feet.

IF YOU THINK YOU'VE BEEN BITTEN:
Go to the hospital within 24 hours and get treated for rabies. Left untreated, rabies is likely to be fatal.

CROCODILE AND ALLIGATOR

DANGER RATING

RISK RATING: ☠ ☠ ☠
Most crocodiles and alligators prefer other foods to humans, but attacks still happen regularly.

SURVIVAL RATING: 25%
If a croc or alligator actually attacks you, you'll need luck and courage to get away.

Crocodiles and alligators are big, dangerous water reptiles with sharp teeth and strong jaws. They live in rivers, lakes, swamps, estuaries, and sometimes even in the sea. Crocodiles, found around the world, have more pointed snouts, while alligators, found mostly in the U.S.A., have wide snouts. Both are dangerous, and they behave in similar ways.

WHAT TO DO

KNOW THE DANGERS:
In an area that has crocodiles or alligators, don't hang around near water. Don't paddle, swim, dangle your feet, or sit on the bank, even if the water looks empty. Crocs like to hide, then zoom out of the water at high speed to grab their prey.

IF YOU SEE A CROC OR ALLIGATOR:
If you're in the water, get out at once and move away. Crocs can swim faster than you. On land, run away fast. If a crocodile or alligator runs after you, keep running as fast as you can, as it will soon get tired.

IF IT CATCHES YOU:
Repeatedly punch the crocodile on the snout and face or hit it with anything in reach, and scream and shout. This may make it let go. If you get free, run away and go to a hospital, since a croc's mouth contains harmful disease germs.

TOP TIP! In cartoons, people sometimes try to wedge a croc's mouth open with a stick. Don't bother trying this—crocodiles and alligators have incredibly powerful jaws and you won't succeed. A punch on the nose will work better.

KOMODO DRAGON

Dragons don't really exist—the Komodo dragon is actually a type of lizard. In fact, it's the biggest lizard in the world, growing up to 10 feet (3 m) long. Komodo dragons live on only a few islands in Indonesia. They hunt large animals such as deer and also feed on carrion, or dead meat. They have a powerful bite that injects their prey with lethal disease bacteria. The bacteria can cause death in about two days. The dragon then comes back to feast on the dead animal.

DANGER RATING

RISK RATING: ☠
Komodo dragons are very rare, so you are not at great risk.

SURVIVAL RATING: 95%
Though they can be deadly, Komodo dragons don't often kill people.

DID YOU KNOW?

If a Komodo dragon is in danger, it can suddenly vomit up its last meal. This reduces its body weight, allowing it to run away more easily.

WHAT TO DO

IF YOU SEE A KOMODO DRAGON:
If you do see one, it will probably be at a zoo or wildlife reserve. Sometimes dragons that are kept illegally, as pets, escape—if you see one on the loose, take shelter indoors and call the police.

ON A TOURIST TRIP:
Tourists are taken on guided tours to see Komodo dragons in the wild. On a trip like this, always stay quiet and calm, and follow your guide's instructions.

IF A KOMODO DRAGON ATTACKS:
As with crocodiles and alligators, try to hit the dragon's nose and head to make it let go. Run away and have any bites treated in a hospital to kill the deadly bacteria.

If you see a Komodo in the wild, never try to feed or touch it.

FUNNEL-WEB SPIDER

The funnel-web spider is found in Australia, and it's one of the most poisonous spiders in the world. There are several species, the most dangerous being the Sydney funnel-web. Most bites happen in late summer, when male spiders are wandering around in search of a female to mate with. They may roam into a house or garage or get trapped in a shed.

WHAT TO DO

BE ON YOUR GUARD:
In eastern Australia, keep a lookout for funnel-web spiders, especially when gardening, hiking, or camping. Learn what the spiders and their webs look like so you'll know what to avoid.

TOP TIP! Always check inside any boots, watering cans, containers, or clothing that has been left outdoors, before you use them. A spider could be hiding inside.

IF YOU ARE BITTEN:
A funnel-web spider bite hurts! You may start to feel sick, dizzy, or tingly. Get to a hospital at once. Keep the bitten body part still. Try to wrap it in a bandage above the bite, and use a splint (a stiff stick) to stop it from moving. For example, for a bite on the hand, wrap the bandage around the arm, starting at the bite and working up to the shoulder. Then tie the splint to hold it straight. If you can, collect the spider safely and take it with you to be identified.

The male Sydney funnel-web spider measures about 1.5 inches (3 cm) long, not including its legs.

BLACK WIDOW SPIDER

Black widow spiders have very poisonous venom. But these are small spiders, with a body length of only about 0.6 inches (1.5 cm), and they cannot inject much venom at once.

Black widows are found in warm countries around the world. They can be killers, but in most cases being bitten by a black widow is unpleasant rather than deadly. Females are much more dangerous than males. Bites usually happen when people disturb black widow webs in woods, garages, or yards at night, when the spiders are active.

DANGER RATING

RISK RATING: ☠ ☠ ☠
Black widow spiders are common and widespread.

SURVIVAL RATING: 95%
Most black widow bites are not fatal.

Most species of black widows are black. Females have hourglass-shaped markings or spots.

WHAT TO DO

SPIDER SENSE:
Black widows come out at night, so avoid stumbling around the garage, yard, or shed in the dark. If you see a black widow, keep your distance and give it time to scuttle away.

IF YOU ARE BITTEN:
Some people do not react much at all to black widow bites, but in most cases the bite will be painful. You should be able to see two tiny fang marks. The poison can cause muscle cramps throughout the body, stomach pain, and vomiting. If you have these symptoms, or think you have been bitten by a black widow, it's always best go to a hospital, even though you may not need antivenom. You can also treat the bite by pressing on it with ice wrapped in a cloth.

HIPPO

Few people realize just how dangerous hippos can be. They seem like slow, lumbering beasts that graze peacefully on the grass or float around in rivers. But hippos are big and powerful, have very sharp teeth, and can run surprisingly fast, reaching speeds of up to 25 mph (40 kph). In Africa, where hippos live, they have claimed hundreds of lives —far more than "fiercer" animals such as lions.

DANGER RATING

RISK RATING: ☠ ☠
Hippos are a risk in Africa, both on land and water, but most people know how to stay safe.

SURVIVAL RATING: 60%
If a hippo decides to charge you, you'll have to run fast to get away.

Hippos spend most of the day in river, coming out at night to feed on grass.

WHAT TO DO

UNDERSTAND HIPPOS:

Hippos are mainly vegetarians and don't want to eat people. They charge if they feel scared or if they are protecting their young. On land, don't get between a hippo and the water, for they like to feel they can reach it at all times. In a boat, be careful not to poke a swimming hippo with your oar—the hippo could upturn the boat and its occupants, or even bite it in two. Always avoid hippos at night, when they are most alert.

CHASED BY A CHARGING HIPPO:

There's no way you can fight a hippo, so start running! Hippos can run fast, but they soon get tired, so you may be able to get away. If you can, go inside a building or a large vehicle, or run among trees or rocks that will slow the hippo down. If the hippo is closing in, you may be able to gain some extra time by changing direction before it reaches you.

DID YOU KNOW?

Hippos are huge! They can grow up to 13 feet (4 m) long and can weigh up to 8,000 pounds (3,600 kg) — as much as 50 grown men.

ELEPHANT

ELEPHANT RAGE

Experts think elephants may be becoming more violent and attacking humans deliberately, in return for our hunting them.

Elephants are the biggest land animals on Earth. A male African elephant can grow to over 11 feet (3.5 m) tall and weigh 16,500 pounds (7,500 kg). Elephants can move fast, too—like hippos, they can run 25 mph (40 kph). So if an elephant charges or attacks, it can be deadly. Female elephants sometimes charge to protect their families, while males can enter a violent state known as "musth." Elephants are responsible for hundreds of deaths every year.

WHAT TO DO

IF AN ELEPHANT CHARGES:

Run away as fast as you can and head for the safety of a strong building, hide behind a large rock, or climb a tall tree. Running in a zigzag pattern may confuse the elephant, and if you are carrying anything, try throwing it off to one side to distract the animal. If the elephant catches you, it may trample you, crush you with its head, or spear you with its tusks. Curl up in a ball, cover your head, and try to crawl or roll to a hiding place.

IN ELEPHANT COUNTRY:

Elephants live in Africa and Asia and are a popular sight for tourists. Never approach elephants on your own—always go with a guided tour.

DANGER RATING

RISK RATING: ☠ ☠ ☠
In countries that have elephants, they are a serious danger.

SURVIVAL RATING: 60%
You can survive being chased and mauled by an elephant.

DOMESTIC DOG

For most people, dogs are loyal friends. But they are descended from wild animals, and they still have natural instincts to hunt and to defend their territory and their puppies. If a dog is angry or scared, it might attack, and because dogs have sharp teeth and strong jaws, they can be dangerous. Millions of people get bitten by dogs every year, and hundreds die from attacks.

Dogs have large, sha teeth, useful in the w for killing their prey.

DANGER RATING

RISK RATING: ☠ ☠ ☠ ☠ ☠
Dogs are everywhere, and you should always regard them as a possible danger.

SURVIVAL RATING: 95%
Most people who are bitten by a dog will survive.

WHAT TO DO

TREAT DOGS WITH RESPECT:

Although dogs can be fun to pet and play with, don't do this with a dog you don't know or with one that is away from its owner. If you want to touch or stroke a dog, always ask the owner first. Stay away from dogs that are guarding their territory—for example in their backyard—and from mother dogs with puppies.

SPOT THE DANGER SIGNS:

If a dog is angry, it may wag its tail very fast, prick up its ears, snarl, growl, or stare at you. Don't look the dog in the eyes, because this makes it feel threatened, and don't run away, for this will make it want to chase you. Stand up tall, stay calm, and tell the dog firmly to go away. Move slowly into a safer position, such as behind some furniture.

IF A DOG ATTACKS:

Curl up in a ball and cover your face and neck with your arms. Lie as still as you can until the dog leaves or help arrives.

DON'T FORGET RABIES!

If you ever get bitten by a dog, you should see a doctor. In many countries, aggressive dogs can be carrying rabies.

PACK OF WOLVES

Wolves are featured in fairy tales as big, bad, and dangerous, but in fact they are less dangerous than pet dogs. These hunters live in packs, and their favorite prey is a weak, sick, or old member of a herd of four-legged animals. Some think wolves avoid humans because we stand on two legs, which reminds them of a bear.

WHAT TO DO

BE WARY OF WOLVES:
Wolves often live in mountainous, forested, or cold parts of the world. Most avoid humans. If you do see wolves, stay away from them, especially if you have a pet dog with you—the wolves may see it as a threat and try to attack it. Stay close to other people.

IF WOLVES ATTACK:
When a pack of wolves finds prey, they will move downwind of their victim, then approach it in single file or spread out to surround it. If you see this happening near you, climb a tree or high rock, get inside a building or vehicle, or stand up tall and raise your arms to scare the wolves away.

A RABID WOLF:
A lone wolf might attack you if it has rabies, for this deadly disease can make animals go crazy and act aggressively. If it pounces, behave as you would for a dog attack.

DANGER RATING

RISK RATING: ☠
Though wolves can kill a human easily, they hardly ever attack people.

SURVIVAL RATING: 70%
If wolves do decide to attack, they are quite dangerous.

DID YOU KNOW?
Wolves don't howl to scare people! They mainly make this sound to call to other members of their pack, or group.

DINGO

A dingo is a type of wild dog found in Australia and Southeast Asia. Dingoes are golden-brown and fluffy and look a lot like friendly pet dogs. But most dingoes are not tame, and they can be extremely dangerous. They are sometimes found in packs, and sometimes alone. Dingoes are most likely to attack young children or to bite tourists who try to feed and play with them.

WHAT TO DO

DINGO SENSE:
In places where dingoes are found, especially Australia, tourists often want to see them in the wild and treat them like pet dogs. Don't do this! Don't try to feed dingoes, pet them, or photograph them up close. Stay together in your group, and never let small children wander off on their own.

IF A DINGO APPROACHES YOU:
Keep an eye on the dingo (or dingoes) and try to stay facing toward it, but don't stare at the dingo since this may be interpreted as a challenge. Fold your arms, stand as tall as you can, and stay calm. Don't scream or shout at first, but if the dingo starts to attack, it may be scared off if you make a sudden loud noise.

IN A DINGO ATTACK:
Unlike some other types of dog, it is possible to scare a dingo away by shouting at it and hitting it. Use any object you may be carrying, such as a stick or an umbrella, to try to defend yourself.

DANGER RATING

RISK RATING: ☠ ☠ ☠
In some parts of Australia, dingoes are common and a well-known risk.

SURVIVAL RATING: 95%
Very few people have died from dingo attacks, though it does happen.

A dingo is similar in size to a large pet dog.

TOP TIP! When camping in a dingo area, you should keep all your food, garbage, and even supplies such as toothpaste wrapped up well and shut away, since they can attract dingoes.

HYENA

Hyenas live in Africa and Asia. They look a bit like dogs, but they have bigger, thicker, longer necks, which contain huge muscles that give hyenas incredible biting power. Their jaws are among the strongest of any animal.

Hyenas usually feed on dead animals, but one type of hyena, the spotted hyena, is a fierce hunter. If hyenas are hungry, they may attack humans. Groups of hyenas have even been known to raid villages.

RISK RATING: ☠ ☠
Hyena attacks are not common, but they are a risk, especially in Africa.

SURVIVAL RATING: 50%
Hyenas are so strong that once they attack, it's hard to escape.

A spotted hyena, the species that is most dangerous to humans.

WHAT TO DO

AVOID THE DANGER:
Hyenas are active mainly at night—don't sleep outdoors or wander around outside in the dark. Listen for whooping or cackling calls that could tell you hyenas are around. Hyenas prefer to attack the young, weak, or sick—keep these people safe.

IF YOU SEE HYENAS:
Always stay away from hyenas unless you are in a secure touring jeep with an experienced guide. If hyenas are approaching you, quickly get inside a car or building or climb a tree before they can surround you.

IF HYENAS ATTACK:
When hyenas attack people, they often lunge straight at the person's neck or head to inflict a deadly bite. You may be able to defend yourself for a few seconds by putting something between yourself and the hyena. If you don't have anything, cover your face with your arms.

DID YOU KNOW? Hyenas use their powerful jaws to munch and crunch up every bit of the animals they eat—including the bones. Most animals gnaw at a bone, but a hyena just crushes it. Even a bear can't do that.

BUFFALO

It's natural to be scared of fierce hunting animals like bears, big cats, and sharks. But would you know to be scared of a buffalo? These large animals are closely related to cows. Like cows, they wander around in herds, munching grass. But if a buffalo is angry, scared, or wounded—or if you get too close to its calf—it can be incredibly dangerous. Buffaloes can charge at high speed, goring (stabbing) their enemies with their huge horns, or trampling them flat.

WHAT TO DO

Buffaloes have huge, sharp, dangerous horns

RESPECT THE BUFFALO: There are several types of buffalo, but the African buffalo is the wildest and most dangerous. It is found across southern and eastern parts of the continent. If you are on a tour, always follow your guide's instructions.

IN A BUFFALO CHARGE: If a buffalo, or a herd of buffaloes, decides to charge at you, it will move slowly at first, giving you some warning. Get inside a building or vehicle, or climb a tree if you can. If it's too late for that, your best chance is to lie down. If you stand up, the buffalo will gore you with its horns, but if you're lying down, it may run past you.

DANGER RATING

RISK RATING: ☠ ☠ ☠
In Africa, buffaloes are a well-known danger and you should always be wary of them.

SURVIVAL RATING: 80%
Buffaloes kill people every year, but if you take care, you should be safe.

A grizzly bear shows off his powerful jaws and sharp teeth.

BEAR ATTACK

Bears are big, strong, and fierce and can be very dangerous. A male grizzly bear can weigh over 600 pounds (270 kg) and stand over 7 feet (2 m) tall on his hind legs.

The greatest danger comes from black bears and grizzly (or brown) bears, found in wild, mountainous areas, and polar bears, which live in and around the Arctic. However, only a handful of people each year actually die from bear attacks.

DANGER RATING

RISK RATING: ☠ ☠ ☠
Actual bear attacks are very rare, but many people do encounter bears while hiking and camping.

SURVIVAL RATING: 90%
In most bear encounters, the bear will give up and go away.

WHAT TO DO

IF YOU SEE A BEAR:
Stay at least 150 feet (50 m) away from the bear. Keep everyone in your group close together. Don't stare at the bear or make it feel trapped. Make noise—talk, whistle, or sing. If the bear knows you're there, it will probably go away.

IF THE BEAR APPROACHES YOU:
Make a loud noise by shouting or banging pots and pans. Make yourself look bigger by waving your arms or lifting your backpack onto your head. Back away slowly, still making yourself look big.

IF THE BEAR CHARGES OR ATTACKS:
Bears often make a bluff charge, then back off. If the bear leaps on you, roll into a ball and protect your head with your arms or backpack. If the bear continues its attack, try hitting its eyes or snout.

TOP TIP! Never run away from a bear! A bear can run faster than you can—up to 30 mph (48 kph).

LION ATTACK

The lion is famous for being fierce. With his huge mane and terrifying roar, the male lion is known as the "king of the jungle." This is mostly a myth. Lions don't live in the jungle at all—they live in grasslands, usually in Africa. Although they can be dangerous, lions kill fewer people than many other wild animals. However, some lions do seem to turn against humans and start hunting them deliberately—and no lion should be considered safe.

DANGER RATING

RISK RATING: ☠ ☠
Lions are fairly rare, so lion attacks are only occasional.

SURVIVAL RATING: 40%
If you're attacked by lions, the chances are they'll win the fight.

Only male lions have the distinctive shaggy mane.

WHAT TO DO

NEVER TRUST A LION:
Lions spend most of the day sleeping. They are most active at night, but they can hunt at any time of day. If you see lions in the wild, stay inside a building or vehicle. People have been attacked when they climbed out of their jeep to take photos. Don't be fooled by a group of lions that seem to be snoozing—they will be watching you carefully and may be considering an attack.

IF LIONS ARE APPROACHING YOU:
Try not to panic and run—move backward and get inside somewhere safe. Be careful, for lions may split up and close in from several sides.

IN AN ATTACK:
It's worth gaining some time by fighting and trying to get away. Yell for help—others may be able to scare the lion away or beat it off.

TOP TIP! If you're viewing lions from a car or jeep, keep the windows closed, and never stick your arms or head out of the vehicle!

TIGER ATTACK

The tiger is the biggest cat in the world. A male can measure up to 12 feet (3.5 m) long from nose to tail. That's as long as a car! Tigers are also immensely strong and can cover as much as 30 feet (9 m) in one leap.

Tigers live in India, China, and other parts of Asia, mainly in grassy or forested areas. They usually hunt wild animals such as wild deer or pigs, but they do sometimes attack humans if food is scarce.

DANGER RATING

RISK RATING: ☠ ☠
Tigers are very rare, and they do not normally think of humans as food.

SURVIVAL RATING: 30%
If a tiger does decide to attack you, it's not good news!

Avoid traveling alone in tiger country!

WHAT TO DO

IF YOU SEE A TIGER:

At first, keep still and quiet. Tigers are more likely to spot you if you move. Wait until the tiger has gone before making your way to safety.

IF A TIGER IS STALKING YOU:

If possible, get into a hiding place such as a vehicle, a hut, or a narrow space between rocks, where the tiger won't be able to reach you. Otherwise, turn to face the tiger, and look as tall and brave as you can. This puts most tigers off, because they like to take their prey by surprise.

IF THE TIGER POUNCES:

If a tiger is leaping through the air at you, figure out where it will land and run to one side, heading for any rocks, trees, or other shelter. If the tiger grabs you, your only hope is for someone to shoot it, beat it off, or scare it away.

PUMA

The puma—also known as the mountain lion, cougar, or catamount—is a big cat found in North, Central, and South America. It has a plain golden-brown or reddish-brown color and is around 2.5 feet (.76 m) tall and 7 feet (2.3 m) long from its nose to the tip of its tail. Although they are not as big as lions and tigers, pumas can be dangerous, especially to children. They sometimes attack hikers, walkers, and villagers in mountain areas, forests, and deserts.

DANGER RATING

RISK RATING: ☠ ☠
Pumas are not likely to attack; they do not usually see humans as food.

SURVIVAL RATING: 70%
Most people can survive a puma encounter, but children are at serious risk if they are attacked.

WHAT TO DO

TAKE CARE IN PUMA COUNTRY:
Watch out for pumas in mountain, scrubland, and forest areas, especially in the western United States and Canada. Never go near a puma kitten or den—a mother puma will defend her babies fiercely.

IF YOU SEE A PUMA:
Don't panic. Look the puma in the eye and back away slowly. Stand tall, raise your arms, and shout loudly to scare the puma. Don't bend down or turn your back to the puma, because this may encourage it to pounce.

IF THE PUMA POUNCES:
Defend your neck and head; the puma will try to bite you here. Fight back, yell, and try to beat the puma off.

Pumas like to jump on prey from trees or high rocks, so watch out!

DID YOU KNOW?

Pumas have very large, powerful back legs and are brilliant at jumping. They can leap as high as 16 feet (5 m) straight up or 33 feet (10 m) horizontally.

WILD BOAR

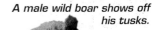

A male wild boar shows off his tusks.

The wild boar is the untamed version of the domestic pig. Pigs themselves can be dangerous, but wild boar are even scarier—they have sharp tusks and teeth and will charge to defend themselves. They can reach up to 7 feet (2 m) in length and weigh up to twice as much as a man. They are found in many parts of the world, including Australia, Europe, Asia, and South America, mostly in forest areas.

DANGER RATING

RISK RATING: ☠ ☠
Wild boars are getting more common, but they won't charge if you leave them alone.

SURVIVAL RATING: 95%
You'll almost certainly survive, but boar attacks can sometimes be deadly due to loss of blood.

WHAT TO DO

BEWARE OF THE BOARS:
Take care in forests if you know wild boars are around, especially at night when they are most active. You are at greater risk if you have a dog, because it may disturb wild boars and make them angry.

IF YOU SEE WILD BOARS:
Wild boars may be found alone or in groups of about 20 made up of mothers and their young. Steer clear of them, especially if you see babies. If boars are about to charge, they will face you, snorting and grunting. Move away fast if this happens.

IF A WILD BOAR CHARGES:
Male boars charge with their heads down, then slash with their large tusks. Females charge with their mouths open, then bite you. Your best strategy is to climb a tree, or run away as fast as you can.

TOP TIP! A boar injured by a hunter or hit by a car can be furious and highly dangerous. If you see one, run away at once.

HORSE

Humans have been training and riding horses for thousands of years. They are among the most important domestic animals in the world. Horses are big and strong, and since they have such close contact with humans, it's no surprise that there are thousands of horse-related accidents every year. A fall from a horse can be very dangerous, especially if you're not wearing a helmet.

WHAT TO DO

MAKE HORSES FEEL SAFE:
Horses may be big, but they are easily scared. Most accidents happen when horses feel trapped or threatened. Always treat horses respectfully and calmly: Never tease them, make them jump, or creep up on them from

Horses may kick and struggle, rear up or run wildly if agitated.

behind. Don't stand behind a horse, or it may kick you, and don't block a horse's path. It's best to stay away from them, unless you know them well or the owner is there.

SPOT THE WARNING SIGNS:
If a horse lays its ears flat against its head, or tosses its head, that may mean it is angry and about to kick or bite.

IF A HORSE RUNS YOU DOWN:
A panicking horse may knock you down or gallop over you. If you fall under a horse, curl up and cover your head—the horse doesn't want to hurt you and will try to avoid you.

TOP TIP! If you have a riding helmet, wear it all the time you are around horses, not just when you're riding. It could protect your head from an unexpected kick.

CHARGING BULL

A bullfighter dodges a bull, using a red cape to distract it.

DANGER RATING

RISK RATING: ☠ ☠
As long as you leave bulls alone, an attack is unlikely.

SURVIVAL RATING: 90%
Bulls do kill people, especially farmers and bullfighters, but it's not common.

A bull is a male cow. Bulls, especially older ones, are often kept on their own in fields. They can be very large and can run fast, so a charging bull can be deadly. As well as chasing and trampling, it can use its horns to gore or throw its victim.

In bullfighting, people tease and taunt a bull. Bulls sometimes kill bullfighters, but the bulls are far more likely to be killed. Bulls will not usually attack you unless you scare them or enter their territory.

WHAT TO DO

DON'T GO THERE:
In the countryside, don't go into any field that has a bull in it—even if the bull is far away. If a field looks empty, check it carefully to be sure.

DANGER SIGNS:
If a bull is angry, it may arch its back, lower its head and sweep it from side to side, and paw at the ground with its hooves. Move away, keeping an eye on the bull, and get to safety as soon as you can.

IF A BULL CHARGES AT YOU:
If you're a long way from safety, the bull will catch up with you. Take off your jacket or top and wave it to one side. As the bull gets closer, throw it away. The bull should run toward it.

RED RAG TO A BULL

According to folklore, bulls are driven mad by the color red. This isn't true—bulls are color-blind. A moving object of any color can make a bull want to charge.

SCORPION

Scorpions are related to spiders. They are usually quite small, ranging from 0.5 inches (1.3 cm) to 8 inches (20 cm) long, and have eight legs. They have two pincers, similar to a lobster's, and a long tail with a stinger at the end. There are over a thousand different species, or types, of scorpion, and most are not dangerous. But a few have very poisonous stingers that can occasionally kill a human.

WHAT TO DO

SCORPION SAFETY:

Scorpions are nocturnal (active at night) so if you're in an area that has dangerous scorpions, sleep under a mosquito net. Check your bed for scorpions before you get in. In the morning, shake out shoes, bags, and clothing in case a scorpion has crept inside.

DANGER RATING

RISK RATING: ☠ ☠ ☠
Scorpions prefer to avoid humans but they are common and will sti if picked up or trodden on.

SURVIVAL RATING: 95%
There's usually time to get to a hospital, so most people survive even dangerous scorpion stings.

IF YOU FIND A SCORPION:

Leave scorpions alone and give them space to scuttle away. You can sweep a scorpion out of a house gently with a broom, but never pick one up. If a scorpion crawls onto your hand or foot, keep the body part flat and shake the scorpion off.

IF A SCORPION STINGS YOU:

If the scorpion is not dangerous, only the area around the sting will hurt. If you start to ache all over, feel sick or dizzy, or have trouble breathing, head for a hospital. If a scorpion stings a small child, or someone who is already unwell, take them to a hospital to get checked out.

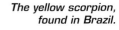

The yellow scorpion, found in Brazil.

DID YOU KNOW? A scorpion cannot harm itself with its sting. It is not affected by its own poison.

KILLER BEES

Honeybees are found all over the world. They help humans by pollinating flowers and making honey. Although they can sting, they usually don't, and for most people a single bee sting is painful but not dangerous.

However, in the 1950s, scientists tried to breed a new type of honeybee that would make extra honey. Instead, they accidentally created an extra-aggressive breed, known as "killer" bees. They are now found in South and Central America, and the southern U.S.A. These bees do not have a worse sting, but they are easily annoyed and often attack in a swarm, which can be deadly.

Killer bees are a type of honeybee, and look just like other honeybees.

DANGER RATING

RISK RATING: ☠ ☠
Killer bees are dangerous, but scientists are working on reducing their numbers and their aggressive tendencies.

SURVIVAL RATING: 90%
Keep a cool head, and you'll probably be able to escape.

WHAT TO DO

DON'T ANNOY THE BEES:
Killer bees are annoyed by people disturbing their nests, sudden movements, and loud noises. Loud yard tools such as chain saws often trigger attacks.

IF KILLER BEES CHASE YOU:
Run as fast as you can and head for a building, a car, or anywhere you can shut yourself inside. Use your clothing to cover as much of your head and face as possible. Don't panic or scream, and don't run into a crowd of people. Don't jump into water, either—you'll have to come up to breathe, and the bees will be waiting.

BEE ALLERGIES Some people are allergic to bee stings. If someone gets stung by a bee and then has trouble breathing, a swollen face or tongue, or collapses, get them to a hospital at once.

CHIMPANZEE

You might think of chimpanzees as cute and cuddly—but you'd be wrong. Some chimpanzees are friendly, but others can be very dangerous.

In the wild, groups of chimps hunt smaller animals such as monkeys. In captivity, chimps have been known to attack people for no obvious reason. A chimp is only about 3 feet (1 m) tall, but it weighs as much as a human, and is up to five times stronger.

A chimpanzee has sharp teeth and a dangerous bite, as well as incredibly strong arms and hands.

DANGER RATING

RISK RATING: ☠
You're unlikely to meet a chimp, except in a secure zoo.

SURVIVAL RATING: 40%
If chimps do decide to attack, it's hard to escape.

WHAT TO DO

TREAT CHIMPS WITH RESPECT:

Even at a zoo, where chimpanzees are safely enclosed, don't annoy them. Don't tease them, throw things, or knock on the glass—just in case they can get out. If you see chimps in the wild, keep clear of them and try not to stare. Don't leave small children alone in chimp areas, or let them go near chimps. If you know someone who has a pet chimp, it's best to keep your distance from it, even if it seems friendly.

IF CHIMPS ATTACK:
If a chimp is coming toward you and trying to attack you, look down and avoid making eye contact. If it attacks, curl up and protect your face, stomach, and head. Call for help so that a zookeeper or park warden can try to save you.

DID YOU KNOW?

In the 1960s, scientist Jane Goodall, famous for her studies of chimps, found out that they are hunters and eat meat as well as other foods. Before this, most people thought chimps were vegetarian.

MOSQUITO

A mosquito is a small buzzing insect, a member of the fly family. It is also the most dangerous animal in the world. Mosquitoes are more dangerous than sharks, bears, tigers, hippos, crocodiles, jellyfish, dogs, and killer bees—all rolled together! Mosquitoes suck blood, and when they bite, they spread deadly diseases, including malaria and yellow fever. Although most of these diseases can be treated, they often strike in poor areas where people cannot afford medicine, so the death toll is very high. Mosquito bites cause around three million deaths each year.

RISK RATING: ☠ ☠ ☠ ☠
In many areas of the world, you're likely to meet a disease-carrying mosquito.

SURVIVAL RATING: 90%
Most people survive mosquito bites, especially if they get treatment in time.

WHAT TO DO

GUARD AGAINST MOSQUITOES:
Dangerous mosquitoes are mainly found in hot, tropical parts of the world, including Africa, southern Asia, and South America. If you are in these areas, you can take special medicines that help prevent malaria. You should also wear insect repellent and cover your arms and legs, especially in the hours of darkness when mosquitoes are active. At night, sleep under a mosquito net.

LOOD SUCKERS

osquitoes don't actually need ood for food. Like butterflies, ey feed on fruit and flower ctar. Only the females suck ood, which they need to help em make their eggs.

IF YOU CATCH MALARIA:
The symptoms of malaria include headaches, feeling very hot and very cold, and feeling sick, dizzy, or tingly. If you feel ill in a tropical country, see a doctor.

A mosquito's body fills up with blood as it sucks from its human host.

SHARK ATTACK

Few things are scarier than the thought of being chased through the water by a terrifying shark, but this image comes mainly from films. In fact, attacks are rare, and sharks are less dangerous than many other animals, including elephants, hippos, or even bees. Most sharks only attack humans because they mistake them for prey, such as seals and penguins.

DANGER RATING

RISK RATING: ☠ ☠
Fewer than 100 shark attacks a year are reported around the world. Half of all shark attacks are reported by surfers.

SURVIVAL RATING: 90%
Despite their fearsome reputation, you will probably escape even if a shark does bite you.

WHAT TO DO

DON'T BE A TARGET:
Don't swim or surf at night, avoid deep water and river mouths, and don't go into murky, frothy water, where a shark could mistake you for a meal. Don't wear anything silvery or sparkly that might look like fish scales.

IF A SHARK APPROACHES YOU:
Keep calm and swim for land. If the shark circles you or bumps you with its nose, stay still and upright, so that it won't think you're a seal. If you're with others, cling together to make a big shape that the shark will not want to approach.

IF A SHARK ATTACKS YOU:
Hit the snout or eyes, or hit it with something, such as a snorkel, to make the shark let you go. Shout for help and try to get ashore, then seek medical help.

DID YOU KNOW? The notorious great white shark is widely feared, but the tiger shark and bull shark are just as deadly and aggressive, with many attacks reported.

PIRANHA SHOAL

Piranhas are fish that live in rivers in South America, such as the Amazon. They have a deadly reputation. In adventure films they hunt in shoals, attacking large animals, such as cows and humans, who have wandered into the water. They are said to bite all the flesh from their victim's bones, churning up the water in a violent "feeding frenzy."

The truth is, they rarely eat people. Piranhas are meat eaters, and they do swim in groups and hunt prey, such as birds, that fall into the water. At certain times of year, however, such as the dry season, they can be very dangerous to humans.

DANGER RATING

RISK RATING: ☠ ☠
If you're in South America, piranhas are a risk, but only a small one.

SURVIVAL RATING: 95%
Few people die from a piranha attack, but these fish give a nasty bite!

Most piranhas are only about 10 inches (25 cm) long, but they are aggressive.

WHAT TO DO

PIRANHA SAFETY:
If you are in South America, avoid going into rivers during the dry season, when the water level falls and hungry piranhas crowd together in schools. If you are swimming, don't splash around—it could make piranhas think you're an injured animal. Don't go into the water if you have an illness or injury. Most people who are attacked by piranhas are thought to get into trouble in the water first and start panicking, attracting the fish.

TOP TIP! Stay away from piranhas on the bank when they have been caught as food. They may still be alive and have a powerful bite—a piranha can bite your finger off.

IF YOU SEE PIRANHAS:
Leave the water if you see piranhas, or if you are warned of sightings. If you are attacked, your best chance is to get out of the water as fast as you can.

STINGRAY

Rays are a type of fish related to sharks. They "fly" along underwater by flapping their wide fins. Stingrays are a group of rays that have a long, sharp, venomous stinger in their tails. If a stingray feels threatened, it can flip its stinger upward suddenly. If you stand on a stingray as it lies on the seabed, or if you swim over the top of one too closely, the stinger could stab you and inject you with poison. The sting is painful, but not usually dangerous.

A southern stingray photographed off the Cayman Islands.

WHAT TO DO

TAKE CARE IN THE WATER:
Stingrays are found in warm, tropical parts of the world, usually in the sea, close to the shore, but also in some rivers. Keep a lookout for stingrays when you are swimming, paddling, snorkeling, or diving.

IF YOU GET STUNG:
Most stings are on the feet or hands. Go back to the shore, and try to get to a hospital for treatment, as parts of the stinger may have broken off under your skin. You can relieve the pain with warm water. Bandage the wound to stop bleeding, if necessary. If you have been stung in the face or body, this could be more dangerous. Do not pull the stinger out, as this could make the wound bleed dangerously. The poison does not usually kill, but the stinger wound can be serious.

TOP TIP! Stingrays often lie flat on the seabed and can be difficult to see. But you can avoid treading on them by shuffling your feet forward through the sand. This will allow a stingray to feel you coming, and it will move away.

SEA SNAKE

Most snakes live on land, but there is a group of snakes that swim in the sea. They look like other snakes, except that the ends of their tails are flattened, like oars, to help them swim. Most sea snakes are very poisonous— their venom is much stronger than that of most land snakes. They usually leave divers and swimmers alone, but they can inflict a deadly bite, especially if they get caught in a fishing net or washed ashore, where someone might tread on them.

DANGER RATING

RISK RATING: ☠
Unless you work on a fishing boat, you will probably not encounter a sea snake.

SURVIVAL RATING: 90%
Even if they bite, sea snakes do not always inject venom, and bites can be treated with antivenom.

WHAT TO DO

IF YOU SEE A SEA SNAKE:
You might see a sea snake while scuba diving or snorkeling, or on the beach, if it has been washed ashore after a storm. Wherever it is, don't touch it. Move away. In the water, sea snakes are curious and often follow divers to look at their equipment. They probably won't bite, but it's best to get away from them if you can.

IF A SEA SNAKE BITES YOU:
You may not feel the bite at first, but if venom has been injected, the poison will soon give you a headache and make you feel sick. Your muscles will start to feel stiff and painful. Gradually, you will feel more and more tired, and it might become hard to breathe. Seek help. There is an antivenom that can stop the worst effects of the poison.

CLOSED NOSE

Sea snakes can't breathe underwater—they have to come to the surface for air. While diving in the sea, they can close their nostrils to keep water out.

BOX JELLYFISH

The box jellyfish is the world's deadliest jellyfish. There are no exact figures, but it is estimated to cause at least 50 deaths per year, mainly in Australia and southeast Asia.

The box jellyfish is large, with a cube-shaped top part up to 10 inches (25 cm) across, and stinging tentacles up to 10 feet (3 m) long. It hunts shrimps and crabs and probably has little interest in humans, but if a swimmer gets caught in its tentacles, it will sting. This jellyfish's sting scars the skin and can stop the heart.

DANGER RATING

RISK RATING: ☠ ☠ ☠ ☠
In Australian and Asian waters, the box jellyfish is common.

SURVIVAL RATING: 70%
Box jellyfish stings are not always deadly, and there are treatments and an antivenom.

WHAT TO DO

STAY SAFE:
In areas that have box jellyfish, don't swim in the sea during jellyfish season (usually the wet season, from October to March). There are often signposts to warn of jellyfish danger. If you do want or need to swim, don't go alone. You can also protect yourself by covering your skin with light clothing, a wetsuit, or a "stingersuit."

DID YOU KNOW?

Some jellyfish stings can be treated by pouring urine onto them! But remember, this doesn't work for box jellyfish stings.

IF YOU ARE STUNG:
A box jellyfish sting is incredibly painful. Yell for help, and call an ambulance. Pour vinegar on the sting (dangerous beaches have a supply of vinegar for this purpose). If the tentacles are stuck to your skin, pick them off with a stick. Try to stay calm while you wait for medical help.

BLUE-RINGED OCTOPUS

The "beak" of a blue-ringed octopus can penetrate a wetsuit.

Compared to most octopuses, the blue-ringed octopus is tiny —small enough to sit in your hand. Yet it it is one of the most dangerous of all sea creatures, with a venomous bite that can kill a human. Its poison works by paralyzing you so that you can't breathe. There is no antivenom—the only treatment is to help the victim breathe until the venom has cleared from his or her body.

DANGER RATING

RISK RATING: ☠☠

Blue-ringed octopuses don't want to bite you—they only will if you touch them or tread on them.

SURVIVAL RATING: 90%

You can survive a bite as long as you know you've been bitten and act fast.

WHAT TO DO

DON'T TOUCH:
Blue-ringed octopuses are found around Australia and in the western Pacific region, usually in rock pools or close to the shore. Never touch any small octopus you find on the beach—even if it doesn't have blue rings. They can change color to blend in with their surroundings, and the blue-ringed octopus's rings only appear when it is alarmed.

IF YOU ARE BITTEN:
You will need help to survive a blue-ringed octopus bite, so don't go to the beach alone! The bite may be painless, but you will soon start to feel numb around the mouth and find it difficult to breathe. Someone must call an ambulance immediately. While you wait for the ambulance, lie down and keep the bitten body part still. Your friends should give you mouth-to-mouth resuscitation.

HUMAN

Since humans arrived on Earth we have built billions of buildings, roads, and railways, and all kinds of transportation devices to get us from A to B. Usually, of course, these things are safe and useful,

DANGERS

but they can be dangerous. Here you can find out what to do if your parachute doesn't open, your ship sinks, or you're trapped in a burning building, a broken cable car, or a sunken submarine.

ON A SINKING SHIP

A large ship or ferry is a very safe place to be. Like a plane, it's safer than a car, a bicycle, or walking around on foot. But any ship can sink—if it hits an iceberg, for example, or gets flooded by a giant wave. To be sure of staying safe, you need to stay calm and listen carefully.

In 1952, Captain Henrik Carlsen stayed with his battered cargo ship, the Flying Enterprise, for seven days.

DANGER RATING

RISK RATING: ☠ ☠
Ships are very safe, but a few do sink each year around the world.

SURVIVAL RATING: 95%
Safety equipment and strategies are designed to keep you as safe as possible if your ship sinks.

TOP TIP! If you do get wet, take your wet clothes off and wrap up in something dry—even if it's just an old coat. Wet clothes will make you lose heat very fast.

WHAT TO DO

IF YOUR SHIP IS SINKING:
Obey the crew's instructions—they are trained in what to do if the ship sinks. They will send for help and arrange for everyone to board a lifeboat. Meanwhile, dress in warm clothes and put on your life jacket.

ABANDONING SHIP:
Don't panic and start fighting for a place on a lifeboat! There will be space for everyone. If you are able-bodied and strong, help children, the disabled, and the elderly to put their life jackets on and get into a lifeboat. Get in carefully yourself and hang on tight!

IN THE LIFEBOAT:
As a ship goes under, it can suck things down with it. So once a lifeboat is full, it should move as far away from the ship as possible. Stay sitting down, and huddle together keep warm.

SUNKEN SUBMARINE

Being deep underwater is dangerous for two main reasons. First, of course, we can't breathe underwater, so those in a submarine or submersible (a kind of minisubmarine) rely on the air supply they take with them. Second, the deeper you go, the more water pressure pushes in on you. In deep oceans, the pressure is so great that it can squash you to death in an instant.

WHAT TO DO

SEND AN SOS:
Unless your submarine is very badly damaged, you should be able to radio a message to rescuers on land, giving them your position.

SAVE OXYGEN:
While you wait, you need to do as little as possible. The less you do, the less of your air supply you'll use up. Sit or lie down, keep warm and talk quietly, read, or sleep.

HOLD OUT HOPE:
Being trapped in a small space is frightening and might make you panic. You need to keep your spirits up and stay calm. Try to comfort and reassure one another, talk about plans for the future, and sing songs to pass the time.

DANGER RATING

RISK RATING: ☠
Not many people will find themselves in this situation.

SURVIVAL RATING: 40%
Survival depends on being rescued, which may not happen in time.

Submarines are built to withstand the huge pressure deep underwater.

ROBOT RESCUE

In 2005, a Russian minisubmarine became trapped underwater when its propellers were caught in fishing nets. Rescuers used remote-controlled robot vehicles to cut the sub free. The seven crew members were saved after three days underwater, with just six hours of air to spare.

TRAPPED IN A SINKING CAR

When you travel by car, you're shut inside a strong, protective box, and strapped in for safety. But if your car lands in water, these safety features become dangerous. The car will sink, and you need to get out quickly. Don't think about taking stuff with you. Concentrate on making sure everyone gets out of the car before it goes under.

DANGER RATING

RISK RATING: ☠ ☠
Driving into deep water isn't very common, though driving over ice increases the risk.

SURVIVAL RATING: 70%
It is often possible to get out, but this is a very dangerous situation.

WHAT TO DO

UNDO YOUR SEAT BELT:
If your car veers off the road and hits water, you'll need your seat belt to lessen the impact. But as soon as the car comes to a stop, make sure everyone's seat belt is undone. Check baby and child seats, too.

OPEN A WINDOW:
The water pressing against the car will make it almost impossible to open the doors. Instead, open the windows fully and climb out. If the windows are electric and aren't working, you'll have to break the glass with your foot or a heavy object. Take care to avoid the broken glass.

IF YOU CAN'T OPEN THE WINDOWS:
Wait inside the car as it fills up with water. Once the car is nearly filled with water, and the air is almost gone, take a deep breath and hold it. You should be able to open a door and escape.

TOP TIP! Once you're free from the car, everyone should cling together and tread water until you have your breath back. Then you can start to yell for help or swim for the shore.

Serious danger: This car has turned upside down in rough water.

BRAKE FAILURE

Cars on expressways and highways drive at high speed. The faster you are going, the longer it will take to stop.

Brakes are there to slow down and stop cars, trucks, buses, and other vehicles. You rely on the brakes to stop at traffic lights, avoid hazards, and turn corners. If your brakes don't work and you can't stop, you're in serious danger of a crash—so all drivers should know what to do. Even if you can't drive yet, it might be worth remembering!

WHAT TO DO

CHECK THE PEDAL:
Often, when a driver can't get the brakes to work, it's because a water bottle, a box of tissues, or some other junk is stuck under the brake pedal. Try to sweep under the pedal with your foot to remove any blockage. Keep trying the brake pedal, for it may start working again. Right away, make sure everyone has their seat belts on.

STEER TO SAFETY:
You need to get away from other cars you could crash into. Signal and move carefully to the side of the road, watching out for pedestrians.

FIND SOMETHING TO SLOW YOU DOWN:
If you are not going too fast—less than 40 mph (60 kph)—use the hand brake to slow you down. You can also try running the car along the edge of the curb or steering it up a hill, if you can do so safely. On country roads, drive off the road onto flat grass or dirt.

TOP TIP! Once you've stopped, don't sit in the car—get everyone out and move them to a safe place while you wait for help.

PARACHUTE FAILURE

DANGER RATING

RISK RATING: ☠
Not many people go parachuting, and if you do, your parachute will almost certainly work.

SURVIVAL RATING: 95%
Stay calm and use your reserve chute, and all should be well.

In the early days of parachute jumping, parachutes failed to open and got tangled up quite often. But modern parachutes are very safe and hardly ever go wrong. If yours does, you will still have a reserve parachute to rely on.

WHAT TO DO

IF YOUR PARACHUTE DOESN'T OPEN:
Don't panic. Take a moment to remember your training, and follow the procedures you have been taught for using your reserve parachute.

IF THE RESERVE CHUTE FAILS, TOO:
This is very unlikely, but it could happen. It is obviously not good news, but people have been known to survive such falls. You may be able to slow yourself down a little by spreading out your arms and legs. You are more likely to survive if you land in bushes or trees, in snow, or on soft, plowed soil.

HITCH A RIDE:
If you have problems while skydiving, you might be able to link on to another skydiver and use his or her parachute. You will have to tie yourselves together, and may be injured while landing.

DID YOU KNOW? Some parachutes have a safety system that can sense if you are close to the ground and falling fast. The reserve chute will open automatically.

STUCK IN A CABLE CAR

DANGER RATING

RISK RATING: ☠ ☠
Cable car catastrophes are pretty rare.

SURVIVAL RATING: 80%
Usually, the car is simply stuck, and you will be rescued.

A cable car soars over Fraser River Canyon in Canada.

Cable cars carry tourists, skiers, and mountaineers up and down mountain slopes. Passengers travel in a hanging car, or a smaller "gondola," which moves up and down a long cable. There are thousands of cable car systems all over the world, and they rarely go wrong. However, cable car accidents can sometimes happen.

CABLE CAR CRASH

A cable car crashed in the Austrian village of Soelden in 2005 after a helicopter passing overhead accidently dropped its cargo of concrete.

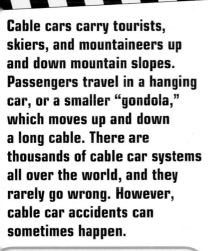

WHAT TO DO

IF YOUR CABLE CAR STOPS:

Don't do anything! Don't panic, run around, or lean out of the windows. Never try to climb out and escape. Sit down—on the floor if there are no seats—and stay calm. You can call for help on a cell phone, but chances are, the cable car control center will know what has happened.

IN HIGH WINDS:

Cable cars can get stuck because of strong winds. In this situation, the car may be blown and shaken about. Stay seated and hold on to something fixed if you can. If the car slides down the cable toward another car, or even falls off the cable, hold on tight, as the impact will shake you even more.

IN A BURNING BUILDING

Every year, thousands of people around the world die in fires in their homes or in other buildings. Some fires are started deliberately, but they often start by accident, too. Fires can be caused by cigarettes, candles, or stoves left burning, or electrical faults. Even fires that seem small can grow very fast and quickly become dangerous.

WHAT TO DO

IF YOU SEE A FIRE:
Back away from the fire and leave the room, closing the door. Everyone should leave the building. If there is a fire alarm, set it off on your way out. Move away from the building, then call the fire department.

IF YOU ARE TRAPPED IN A BURNING BUILDING:
Move away from the flames, closing doors behind you to slow down the spread of the fire. If you can use a phone safely, call the fire department. Go to a room with a window, open the window if you can, and wave and call for help. Don't climb out unless you are close to the ground. If fire or smoke gets into the room, stay beside the window and lie on the floor, as the heat and smoke will rise.

DANGER RATING

RISK RATING: 💀💀💀💀
Fire is a common danger and can affect any building. Smoke alarms save lives every year—get one.

SURVIVAL RATING: 90%
Staying calm, calling for help, and getting out fast will give you a very good chance of survival.

TOP TIP!
If you're stuck in a building that's on fire, it may seem like a good idea to break the windows, but try to avoid this. The glass could fall down onto rescuers and survivors on the ground and cause terrible injuries.

BROKEN POWER LINE

In most places, power lines carry electricity high above our heads. The high-voltage electricity is dangerous, but normally way out of reach. However, high winds, an ice storm, an earthquake, or sometimes even a helicopter or plane accident, can cause power lines to break and come snaking to the ground. They may still be live with electricity and can be very dangerous indeed.

DANGER RATING

RISK RATING: ☠ ☠
Power lines are usually only a danger during severe storms.

SURVIVAL RATING: 95%
Get away from the line, and you'll be safe.

WHAT TO DO

IF YOU SEE A FALLEN POWER LINE:

First, stay away from it and don't touch it. Sometimes broken power lines shoot out sparks and snake around, so you must keep away. Even if the power line is still, and looks dead, leave it alone just in case.

IF A POWER LINE FALLS ON YOUR CAR:

The electricity could flow through the metal parts of the car. Stay inside, don't touch the car doors, and call for help.

IF THE POWER LINE TOUCHES SOMEONE:

You need to get the power line off them, but don't touch the line or the person yourself. Use a wooden or plastic object, such as a stick or traffic cone, to push the power line away. Then drag the person to safety and call an ambulance.

In July 2005, Hurricane Dennis brought down electricity pylons all over the island of Cuba, making it very dangerous to move in the wet streets.

FALLEN DOWN A MINE SHAFT

The entrance to an abandoned mine shaft in Somerset, England.

DANGER RATING

RISK RATING: ☠ ☠
Mine shafts are very dangerous, ▌
you are quite unlikely to fall into o▐

SURVIVAL RATING: 30%
Deep mine shaft falls are
often deadly.

A mine shaft is a deep, narrow hole in the ground, leading to an underground mine. At large, working mines, the entrances to mine shafts are surrounded by buildings and safety fences, so they are not usually dangerous. The biggest danger comes from abandoned mines in the countryside, especially small ones that were dug a long time ago.

WHAT TO DO

IF YOU FALL INTO A MINE SHAFT:

Many abandoned mine shafts are overgrown with bushes—so if you feel yourself falling, you might be able to grab at plants to drag yourself out. If you do fall down, protect your head with your arms, and hope it's not deep.

AT THE BOTTOM:

If you're awake, that's a good sign. Moving slowly and carefully, as you may be injured, try to get to one side of the shaft, so that you are not under the entrance. That way, if anyone else falls in, they won't land on you. Rescuers might also dislodge rocks as they enter the shaft to find you. Yell for help, or use a cell phone to call for help.

BEWARE OF WATER

Some mine shafts have pools of water at the bottom. If there is water, try to move away from it.

HOW DEEP?

People who fall down mine shafts typically fall about 60 to 70 feet (20 m). However, some mine shafts are much deeper—330 feet (100 m) deep, or more. That's like falling off a 30-story building.

TRAPPED IN A GRAIN SILO

Grain might not seem all that scary. But serious accidents can happen on farms when large amounts of grain are being stored, transported, or poured from one container into another.

A grain silo, or grain bin, is a huge grain container, usually several stories high. If you are inside one, you can get trapped. Moving grain can suck you down and suffocate you.

DANGER RATING

RISK RATING: ☠ ☠
This is only a major risk on farms. Stay away from silos to be safe.

SURVIVAL RATING: 50%
When grain silo accidents happen, they're often serious.

When grain is poured, it acts like water, so you can sink into it.

WHAT TO DO

STAY AWAY:
First of all, never go near grain silos, grain bins, or grain transporters of any kind—unless you are the farmer and know what you are doing.

IF YOU FALL INTO GRAIN:
If the grain is not moving, you should be able to stand on it without sinking. Stay near the walls, because a "bridge" or crust of grain can form in the middle of the silo, covering a gap below. You could fall in and get covered with grain. Keep calm and call for help.

IF YOU SINK UNDER THE GRAIN:
Grain that is being poured or moved can suck you under and hold you tight. You can also get covered in grain if you fall through a grain bridge, or if a heap of grain collapses on you. If this happens, stay calm and hold your arms in front of your face to make a breathing space as you sink.

TOP TIP! If you or someone else is buried in grain, don't give up hope. People can sometimes survive for hours before being rescued, if they have space to breathe.

BRIDGE COLLAPSE

Bridges are designed to stay up. Scientists, engineers, and architects calculate very carefully how strong and what shape and size a bridge has to be, and what materials to use. But it can go wrong. A mistake in the plans or in the work, unexpected freak weather, too much weight on the bridge, or damage caused by age can all lead to a bridge collapse.

DANGER RATING

RISK RATING: ☠
Bridges collapse now and again, but there's only a very small chance you'll be involved.

SURVIVAL RATING: 70%
Bridges often fall apart quite slowly, giving people a chance to escape.

WHAT TO DO

AVOID BRIDGE BUILDING SITES:
If a bridge is going to go wrong, it often does so at an early stage, during the building work. Avoid going near or under bridges that are being built, just in case.

A bridge collapsed in Nanhai, China, after a boat crashed into it.

IF A BRIDGE STARTS TO WOBBLE OR CREAK:
Before a bridge actually collapses, there may be several warning signs. It might creak, wobble, sway, bend, or crack. If you see or hear any of these things, get off the bridge immediately, or move out from under it. People have survived bridge collapses by leaving their cars and running off bridges. Based on the traffic, you'll have to decide if this is a good idea, or if you can get off the bridge more quickly in a vehicle.

IF THE BRIDGE FALLS:
If you're on foot as the bridge falls, hold on tight—cling to the bridge railing or cable, since it may stay attached. If you're in a vehicle, make sure your seat belt is buckled and bend forward to shelter from impact and flying glass.

TOP TIP! After you land on the ground or in water, move away from the bridge fast, because more vehicles and debris may fall on you.

PLANE CRASH

Many people don't like flying. But did you know that planes are incredibly safe and crash very rarely? You're safer on a plane than you are in a car, or even in your house. Even when planes crash, most passengers usually survive. Some plane accidents happen on the ground, and a lot of the passengers escape. Others happen when the plane goes wrong in mid-air, but the pilot may be able to make a crash landing.

This plane overshot the runway and crashed in Toronto in 2005. It caught fire, but all 309 passengers survived.

DANGER RATING

RISK RATING: ☠
Your chance of being in a plane crash is very small indeed.

SURVIVAL RATING: 90%
It might seem incredible, but over 90% of people involved in plane accidents do survive.

WHAT TO DO

BRACE! BRACE!

If the pilot or crew on a plane tell you to "Brace!" it means you should lean forward, with your head either resting on your knees or leaning against the seat in front. In a crash, this position helps to keep you still and avoid flying debris.

GET OUT FAST:

Always listen to the crew's instructions. Once the plane has come to a stop, get out, since the plane may catch fire. Undo your seat belt (remember it does not work like a car seat belt) and head for the nearest exit. If the plane is already on fire, crawling along the floor will help keep you away from the heat, smoke, and fumes.

ONCE YOU'RE OUT:

Follow the crew's instructions for getting down a safety ramp. Check yourself for injuries—in the shock of the crash, you may not have noticed them. Once you're away from the plane, sit down and wait for rescuers.

TOP TIP! You'll be more likely to survive a crash if you plan an escape when you board. Count the seats between you and the exit, so you can feel your way in the dark.

ACKNOWLEDGMENTS

The publisher thanks the following agencies and illustrators for their kind permission to use their images.

Cover: tl Corbis/Renee Lynn, tr Science Photo Library/ Fred K. Smith, bl Corbis/Theo Allofs, br Joanne Cowne

Photos: Pages 1 Photodisc; 2–3 Yellowstone National Park, Corbis/Tim Davis; 4–5 Corbis/ Meijert de Haan/EPA; 6–7 Corbis/Fabrice Coffrini; 8–9 Corbis/Michael S. Yamashita; 10–11 Photodisc; 12 Lyn Topinka/USGS, inset Corbis/Bettmann Archives; 13 Rex/Sipa Press; 14 FLPA; 16 Corbis/TWPhoto; 17 Reuters/ Stringer; 18tl David Rydevik; 18tr Nature/ Photodisc;18br Corbis/Ashley Cooper; 19t Science Photo Library/David A Hardry/Futures; 20 BBC Photo Library, London; 21t Corbis/ Ralph A. Clevenger; 21b Corbis/Lake County Museum; 22 Corbis/Michael Hanschke/dpa; 23t Corbis/Mike Theiss/Ultimate Chase; 23b Corbis/ Reuters; 24t Rex Features/RS/Keystone USA; 24b Corbis/Bettmann Archive; 25 Rex Features; 26 Corbis/Thierry Orban; 27t Corbis/Layne Kennedy; 28 Yellowstone National Park; 29 Corbis/Simela Pantzartzi/EPA; 30 Corbis/Tony Arruza; 31 Corbis/Jim Zuckerman; 32 Getty Images/Martin Baumann/AFP; 33 Corbis/Larry W. Smith/EPA; 34 Corbis/Eric Nguyen; 35t Corbis; 35b Corbis/Chris Collins; 36 Corbis/ Michael Freeman; 37 Corbis/Andrew Brown/ Ecoscene; 38 Corbis/Carol Hughes/Gallo Images; 39t Corbis/Meijert de Haan/EPA; 39b Corbis/Chris Hellier; 40 Corbis/Scott Stulberg; 41 Nebojsa Kovacevic; 42 Corbis/Jenifer Brown/ Star Ledger; 43 Corbis/Karen Kasmauski; 45 Corbis; 46 Corbis/Galen Rowell; 47 Corbis/ Jerome Minet/Kipa; 48 Corbis/Ashley Cooper; 49t Corbis/Uli Wiesmeier; 49b Corbis/Charlie Munsey; 50 Corbis/SYGMA; 51 Corbis/Tobias Bernhard/Zefa/Corbis; 52 Kaj Sorensen; 53t Corbis/Momatiuk–Eastcott; 54 Nature/Pete Oxford; 55 Corbis/John Van Hasselt; 58t Corbis/Peter Johnson; 58b Corbis/Ryan Pyle; 59 Nature/Photodisc; 60t Corbis/Darren Staples/Reuters; 60b Corbis/Karen Kasmauski; 61t Corbis/Christopher Morris; 61b Nature/ Photodisc; 62 Corbis/Tom Bean; 63 Corbis/ Galen Rowell; 64t Corbis/Kevin Schafer; 65 Corbis/John Carnemolla; 67b Corbis/Joe McDonald; 68 Corbis/Martin Harvey; 69 Corbis/ Martin Harvey; 70t Photodisc; 71 Corbis/Theo Allofs; 72t Corbis/Gary W. Carter; 72b Corbis/ Joe McDonald; 73 Corbis/Buddy Mays; 74t Rex Features/Karen Paolillo; 74b Corbis/Arthur Morris; 75t Rex Features/Sipa Press; 76 Rex Features/DPPI; 77 Corbis/Tim Davis; 78 Rex Features/James D. Morgan; 79 FLPA/David Hosking; 80t Photodisc; 80b Yellowstone National Park; 81t Corbis/Renee Lynn; 82 Photodisc; 83 Photodisc; 84 Corbis/Frank Lukasseck; 85 Rex Features/Nature Picture Library; 86 Corbis/Lothar Lenz; 87 Rex Features/Patrick Frilet; 89 Corbis/Kevin Schafer; 90 Rex Features/Nature Picture Library; 91 Rex Features/CDC/Phanie; 93t Science Photo Library/Peter Scoones; 93b Corbis/Reuters; 94 Rex/Jo Mahy/Splashdown Direct; 95b Rex Features/Nature Picture Library; 96 Rex Features/Nature Picture Library; 97 Corbis/ Jeffrey L. Rotman; 98–99 Corbis/Zefa/Markus Moellenberg; 100 Corbis/Bettmann; 101 Rex Features; 102 Rex Features/Ken McKay/Andrew Murray; 103 NPS photo/Harlan Kredit; 104t Rex Features/DPPI; 105t Corbis/Paul A. Souders; 105b Getty Images/AFP/Johannes Simon; 106 Corbis/Bill Stormont; 107 Corbis/ Alejandro Ernesto; 108 Rex Features/Bob Bowen; 109 Photodisc; 110 Rex Features/Sipa Press; 111 Rex Features/Keystone

Illustrations: Pages 15 Gill Tomblin/Simon Gurr; 19b Nick Tibbott; 27b Cecilia Bandiera; 44 Gill Tomblin/Simon Gurr; 53b Nick Tibbott; 56–57 Gill Tomblin/Simon Gurr; 64b Joanne Cowne; 66t Alan Male; 66b Gill Tomblin/Simon Gurr; 67t Alan Male; 70b Gill Tomblin/Simon Gurr; 75b Gill Tomblin/Nick Tibbott; 81b Nick Tibbott; 88 Alan Male; 92 Gill Tomblin/Nick Tibbott; 95t Alan Male; 104b Simon Gurr